HORSE SHOW JUDGING *for* BEGINNERS

Also by the author:

SHOWING FOR BEGINNERS

HORSE SHOW JUDGING *for* BEGINNERS

GETTING STARTED AS A HORSE SHOW JUDGE

HALLIE I. McEVOY

The Lyons Press
Guilford, Connecticut
An Imprint of The Globe Pequot Press

10 9 8 7 6 5 4 3 2 1
ISBN 1-58574-466-2
Printed in the United States of America

Library of Congress Cataloging-in-Publication data is available on file.

CONTENTS

DEDICATION

To Trudy Cohen, my dear friend and the first person I ever judged with;
to Joan Starck, a wonderful person who truly understands
what showing is all about;

And to Thom—always and forever.

ACKNOWLEDGMENTS

SINCE THE PUBLICATION OF MY FIRST BOOK (*Showing for Beginners*) in 1996, I've heard over and over again, "When does your next book come out?" I'd like to thank everyone for their patience while I dithered about writing another book, and I'd like to express my gratitude to everyone who kicked me in the butt to get going on this volume.

As with any project, there are numerous people who deserve a mention. Judges and stewards Victor Hugo-Vidal, Cornelia Lacy Herrick, Rita Timpanaro, Don Tobey, Jackie Martin, and Lilli Bieler have all contributed substantially to my style and views of judging. Licensed officials Eric Straus, Judy Richter, Dave Johnson, Jane Dow, Ann Jamieson, Amy Theurkauf, Kim Ablon-Whitney, Randy Neumann, and Sherry Robertson provided great insights and shared crucial advice for beginner judges.

The staff, students, and horses at SUNY Morrisville College Equine Program have earned a special place in my heart for their willingness to answer questions and model for photographs. Special thanks to James Hastie, Bonnie Miller, Lisa Eklund, Bill Maddison, Julie McClain, Kim Asher, Joe Bubbles Star, and Calvin.

I've been lucky enough to work with some exceptional horse people over the past few years. In particular, Kim Johansen of The Livery Horse Center is always willing to listen to my thoughts and offer suggestions; Ellen and Marc Gabes of Running Horse Farm always have something new in store for me when I judge for them; Virginia Rice of the Rice Farms and Winner's Circle Horse Shows continues to encourage and inspire me; Kim Irish Bisson of Cedar Ridge Farm is generous in her advice about all topics related to horses; top dressage rider Kenn Acebal has shared many insightful comments with me over the years; the late Robert Hoskins always encouraged me whether he knew it or not; and Lee Krantz Connelly started me out in the right direction long ago.

Friends and family Elaine Pollak, Inge and Werner Hotrich, Jane Norrie, Sandy and Louie Dota, Bernie Cohen, Herb Starck, Joyce Bennett, Kerin Stackpole, Mike and Debra Lischin, Kathy Schwartzman, Stacey Wigmore, Karen Anderson, DVM, Kate Rogers, Paula and Gunther Hertwig, Heidi Hertwig, Hope and Ken Barry, Kristin Maslack and Rio, Robin Yandell and Chester, and Fran Fitzgerald and Galen have been a constant source of strength, inspiration, and focus.

Gratitude is also due to Steve Price, my editor, who has amazing patience and keen insight into writing about horse topics. Someday I hope to be as well published as Steve.

A special thank-you to the horses in my life, and to Cookie, my canine companion who accompanies me on the road. I couldn't have done it without you, Cookie!

F O R E W O R D

by Victor Hugo-Vidal

WHEN HALLIE ASKED ME TO WRITE the foreword for her new book on judging, I couldn't wait to read the text. It seems she asked me before the book was written, so I was held in tantalizing limbo for quite some time. It finally arrived and was worth the wait—it surely does not disappoint!

After my first read of the book, it made me think back and realize two things. First, how the AHSA (I can never come to call it by its new name, USA Equestrian—I've become a creature of habit!) has changed since I first got my judge's license. There was no Licensed Officials Committee (which I now serve happily on) in those "good old days," and the horse show world was small enough so that word of mouth and three references sufficed! How we've progressed. Second, the horse show world in general has changed, specialized, and grown, and also lost some of the fun, replaced by seriousness and much higher expenses along the way.

To let everyone know how long I've been doing this judging thing, my AHSA/USAE number is 155. Everyone else's numbers now seem to be five or six digits. Many stewards and technical delegates accuse me of lying, or at least fibbing, and the tactful ones say I must be forgetful and am only giving them part of my number!

However, with the growth of the sport and the number of licensed officials, something had to be done. And it was, and the system sure has come a long way. Consequently, there is a good reason for this book, which helps you through the labyrinth of the jungle of getting your license.

I grew up in a lighter and more flexible era when many felt they had to help the next generation. It was long before the days of computers, faxes, and e-mail, and even before answering machines.

Things seemed much easier and slower then; but this is now and I shouldn't reminisce too much, except to say I owe my reputation to all those wonderful judges who so patiently answered all my naive and probing questions, before the days of the rule that you *must* go through the steward to speak to the judge (I think that rule was made because of me!).

I will not list all of the many, many wonderful women and men whom I tortured at the lunch recess or after a long grueling show—we stood on our feet all day to judge back then—or even after a potty break. Most all have gone to heaven (not because of me), but I hope this gives them a laugh or two. The road to knowledge is never-ending and traveled too slowly, but those resourceful and mostly nice people helped me to become wiser and brighter, and I give them all my profuse thanks.

What makes a good judge? I cannot give the definitive answer, but only my opinion after many, many shows of varying types and degrees, held in weather that has run the gamut from glorious to disastrous, but mostly somewhere in between.

A love of the horse and of equitation starts off my list. Patience (the hardest for me to learn!) comes next. A good sense of humor is most helpful, especially when everything is going wrong around you—or worse, not going at all. Knowledge of what you're judging, with the ability to rank mistakes in order, as well as placing best to worst, and doing so quickly. You must remember not to overwork horses or riders. A workable set of judging symbols (hieroglyphics) holds you in good stead, and "the less you write, the less you miss" are wise words to remember.

It's important to make your decisions and not vacillate or question yourself. Having a tough hide, like an elephant or a rhinoceros, is helpful. Remember, judging is not a popularity contest—only the blue-ribbon winner is guaranteed to go away happy. The poor losers, ignorant professionals, overly proud parents, and others will try to blame the dumb (and worse adjectives!) judge. Stand proud, shrug it off, and remember—it's only you who has to look into the mirror at night.

Being courteous and pleasant and suffering fools gladly will always help keep your reputation shiny. Don't be overbearing or supercilious. Above all, don't give the impression of being a know-it-all and talking down to people. I learned that the hard way. Smiles and compliments go a long way toward soothing irate exhibitors who come to talk to you before they've cooled down.

Remember, you have been invited to give your opinion. The exhibitors have hopefully read the prize list and know that you are judging. If they can't take the results and think you're a crook or, even worse, ignorant or blind, don't be afraid to use a line I've made up over the years: "Please, if you see my name on the judging panel in the prize list, do yourself and me a favor and choose another show!" You just can't please everyone all of the time.

Now, why judge? For me, it is a place I love to be, and where I am most content and happy. I've had my fifteen minutes of fame as both trainer and rider. As a Libra, I love weighing good and bad and solving math problems while judging. I would rather be at a horse show, preferably well run and under good conditions, than anyplace else I can think of.

I love watching the good and the talented in our sport (doing well as well as making mistakes), and I love finding new "diamonds in the rough" and giving them their start. I love pinning the steadfast old trooper over the quality animal when the trooper outperforms him, or rewarding the rider with good habits, gleaned through lots of practice, over the obviously talented and gifted rider who has made an error. That's what competition is all about, and that's why each class is a clean sheet of paper to mark up and come out with a new set of results.

To me, it is fun to see the horse that started out spooking and stopping finally have faith enough in his rider to get around passably enough to achieve a prize. Or the rider, young or old, who finally has enough faith in him- or herself to realize he or she can get the job done and be rewarded for it. These are judging's small, subtle pleasures for me, which are just as important as crowning a national champion.

If you have the ability to sit in one place for a long time, the stamina to put up with long days (sometimes under very trying conditions), the love of the sport, the ability to be chastised and screamed at when you know you are right, the knowledge of the rules and the ability to sort things out, the ability to live with yourself without a need of anyone to talk to, to not eat or drink for long periods of time, then you might savor judging. Give it a try; it is very rewarding. What is the ultimate reward for judging? I think it is to have on your tombstone HE WAS FAIR.

If you want to know how to start, this book is the answer.

Enjoy . . .

Introduction: Why Judge?

To **BECOME A LICENSED JUDGE** you need several important attributes. No matter which division you wish to judge—Western, Reining, Hunters, Jumpers, Welsh, Combined Training, Dressage, Arabians, Saddlebreds, Shetlands, or any other—you must have incredible drive, a strong sense of balance and fairness, and an even temper combined with a thick hide.

A strong foundation of knowledge in your chosen field is also a prerequisite, along with a continuing desire to further your equine education. It is also necessary to stay up to date with the current trends and rules in your chosen association as well as other breed and judging organizations. Most importantly, though, judging is not a profession for the faint of heart.

Officiating at horse shows and events can be rewarding, wonderful, and fun. It can also be aggravating, difficult, and boring. Your preparation and attitude are the keys to ensuring a positive outcome. You cannot control the organization of the event, the personality of your fellow workers, or the weather. You can, however, modify your own attitude and adjust pleasantly to even the most adverse circumstances.

Each individual has his or her own reasons for becoming a horse show judge. You should be motivated by the love of the sport, and the lure of watching fine horses and talented riders perform. Some professional judges want to give back to the sport in which they have made their livelihood.

It is important to note that the need for qualified officials continues to grow each year. With the boom in horse shows, some competitions have trouble finding capable judges. One of the reasons is that many judges are also trainers (it is almost impossible to make a living just judging horse shows), and trainers don't want to give up a day or a week of coaching their students at a show in order to judge.

This last reason comes into play for the judge/trainer who takes his or her students to a show circuit that lasts for consecutive weeks. If you and your students are at a show grounds for six weeks of shows, it is literally impossible to walk away from your students for one of those weeks to judge instead of coach. Why? Because according to most organizations' licensed officials rules, to judge someone with whom you have a current business relationship is considered a conflict of interest. That would mean all your students would have to skip one week of showing, and that would not make them happy.

The answer to this quandary is that more people need to be licensed to judge. Although this situation is not ideal for current judges and competitors, it does give aspiring judges an open door to walk through if they work hard and pay their dues.

Do you need to be a great rider to become a judge? Not necessarily. Not every top rider or trainer makes a good judge; judging takes a different type of talent and personality. Many average riders have gone on to become top judges. Although you do not need to be a great rider, you do, however, need to be a better-than-average horseman.

An aspiring judge must decide if his or her motivations match the reality of the position. If you are looking for glamour, fame, and high pay, look for another vocation. Long hours, hard work, and horse show food (hot dogs, french fries, warm soda, and other items filled with fat, sugar, and sodium) are the realities of judging. At many shows you can't even expect a lunch break. I've been known to choke down a hamburger while horses whirl around me during a flat class.

Fame and fortune come to only a few judges after many years perfecting their craft. Are you looking for opportunities to observe wonderful horses and riders, to enjoy satisfaction with a job well done, or to further your equine education? If so, judging is for you.

Many judges approach each show they officiate with a deadly serious attitude, rather than anticipation and joy. This is not to say

Judith Buck Photo

Rodney Jenkins and Idle Dice

that judging is to be taken lightly; rather, it should be kept in perspective. What you do when judging a horse show will not affect world peace, cure cancer, or make you rich. An overbearing and stiff attitude will get in the way of your personal enjoyment and not improve your judging one whit.

You can accomplish several important things when judging. You can encourage beginner riders, expand your equine knowledge, make new friends, and watch fine horses compete. Should you have the honor of judging a large national show, relish the opportunity and proudly represent the organization that has granted you a license. But above all, remember your love of horses and your enjoyment of the sport—the reasons you wanted to judge in the first place.

The idea of becoming a Hunter and Equitation judge first occurred to me in the 1970s while watching the legendary show hunter Ruxton and such show jumpers as Rodney Jenkins, Michael Matz, and Michelle McEvoy Grubb compete. To judge such dynamic horses and riders seemed to me to be a privilege and rare honor. Over the years I have seen every type of horse and pony imaginable, and I have learned something from every one of them.

While judging, I have been stepped on, bitten, slimed, and kicked. I have ended up sunburned, soaking wet, and freezing cold—sometimes all in one day. I have even managed to fall out of a judges' stand on more than one occasion. Competitors have ambushed me at my car to ask why I did not pin their obviously lame horse. Despite all this, judging is by far the most rewarding experience I have ever had working with horses and people.

The judging pleasure I receive during the course of an average show is staggering. The smile of a young beginner who finally manages to get a thirty-year-old pony to canter or lope; the elegance of a promising Equitation rider; the brilliance and style of a Conformation Hunter; the thrill of seeing a perfect Western Pleasure horse . . . no other experience can compare to a day as a horse show judge.

Note: This book is not designed to be the definitive guide to judging; rather, it is meant to introduce you to the basic requirements of judging Hunter Seat and Stock Seat riders as well as horses. Please do not approach any judge and announce, "It isn't that way in Hallie's book." You won't earn any brownie points.

Types of Shows

ONE OF THE WONDERFUL THINGS about our equestrian sport is the great diversity of breeds and disciplines. Almost every breed association has competitions that showcase its animals. Disciplines such as Hunters/Jumpers or Reining have shows that feature only their style of riding. Additionally, there are different types of shows within each category—recognized, unrecognized, discipline-specific shows, breed shows, open shows, schooling shows, Intercollegiate shows, and shows for riders with disabilities.

Let's take a look at the different types of shows you may encounter.

RECOGNIZED SHOWS

The term *recognized* covers a broad spectrum. Generally, it means that a show is affiliated with a specific discipline or breed organization, and that points earned at the competition can count for year-end awards. Although most recognized shows are run by private management teams, the show managers must adhere to strict rules concerning the conduct of the competition that are provided and promulgated by the governing organization.

When a show is recognized, there are firm guidelines that the show management must follow in terms of hiring licensed officials, the safety of the facility, the footing provided, the number and size of warm-up rings, whether emergency medical technicians (EMTs) must be on the grounds, and many other areas. It is in the best interest of the horse show to adhere to these rules, not only to attract exhibitors, but also to keep its recognized rating.

Dozens of breed, discipline, and regional organizations sanction recognized shows, and on any given weekend you can find a plethora of events. Some organizations that sanction recognized shows include USA Equestrian (USAE—formerly the American Horse Shows Association), the American Quarter Horse Association (AQHA), the American Paint Horse Association (APHA), the National Reining Horse Association (NRHA), the American Driving Society (ADS), and the U.S. Dressage Federation (USDF), among many others. Even the National Miniature Donkey Association (NMDA) has recognized shows.

In order to judge a show recognized by a specific organization, you must be a licensed judge with that organization. We'll discuss the licensing procedure in chapter 2.

UNRECOGNIZED SHOWS

Although there are thousands of recognized shows each year, many more are unrecognized shows. An unrecognized show is similar to a recognized show in that one discipline or breed may be featured; points from the show, however, will not count toward national year-end awards.

Many show managements run unrecognized shows as a stepping-stone to recognized shows. Most riders are more comfortable starting their show career at an unrecognized or schooling show, hence the need for these types of competitions. Also, in an unrecognized competition, show management need not adhere to the regulations that apply to recognized shows. For instance, you don't need to hire a steward or file results with a governing organization. For these reasons, it is much easier in terms of needing less labor to run an unrecognized show.

Some unrecognized shows are run just like recognized shows, in that licensed judges are hired and the show schedule offers similar classes. Unrecognized shows can be used by riders as preparation for the bigger recognized shows, or may be attended just for the joy of showing.

Because unrecognized shows are not regulated by a governing organization, their quality can vary widely. Before judging an unrecognized show, check with friends or trainers who have attended the show in the past. In that way you can ascertain if the competition is managed and run well. This is very important when you are judging due to the number of issues (*Is the secretary organized? Is sufficient help to run the show available? Is the footing safe for the horses?*) that can arise during a typical show day.

I've judged some wonderful unrecognized shows that featured superb management, excellent show grounds, and a superior caliber of competitor. Unfortunately, I have also judged unrecognized shows that adhered to no recognizable set of rules, were managed poorly, and offered neither food nor bathroom breaks. For these reasons, many licensed judges will not judge unrecognized shows.

When I am approached about officiating at an unrecognized show, I grill the show manager or secretary. *What are the grounds like? How long has this show existed? Who has judged here in the past? How much will I be paid? Will there be EMTs on the grounds?* These are all details to be taken into consideration.

DISCIPLINE AND BREED SHOWS

As the names imply, these shows feature a specific discipline or equine breed. They can be either recognized or unrecognized. Some examples of discipline shows are Hunter/Jumper, Dressage, Reining, Saddle Seat, and Western. Breeds such as Morgans, Arabians, Quarter Horses, Paints, Welsh Ponies, and many others are featured in breed shows.

Examples of large discipline shows include Dressage at Devon in Pennsylvania and the Hampton Classic Horse Show in New York (Hunters and Jumpers). What is interesting about discipline shows is that you can see many different breeds competing in the same style of riding.

Conversely, the breed shows only spotlight one breed, but often display that breed's versatility in different disciplines and divisions. One of the biggest breed shows, the American Quarter Horse Congress, showcases thousands of American Quarter Horses in a variety of disciplines. At the congress you can see American Quarter

Horses shown as Hunters and Jumpers, in Driving classes, shown in-hand in Conformation/Halter classes and in Showmanship classes, and as Western Pleasure and Equitation horses.

OPEN SHOWS

Open shows are just what the name implies—open to many different disciplines and breeds. My favorites include Washington County Field Days in East Montpelier, Vermont, and the Lancaster Fair Horse Show in Lancaster, New Hampshire.

One of the most unusual classes at the Lancaster Fair Horse Show is Draft Horses Under Saddle. Bear in mind that your average draft horse, whether Belgian or Percheron, is most often driven, not ridden. Many of the drivers unhitch their draft horses, find some saddles that might fit (extra-wide trees are needed), and throw a willing rider on board. Since many of the draft horses are used to working in pairs, they will often "buddy up" with another horse as they are ridden around the ring. As a judge, you are then confronted with dozens of draft horses glued to a friend as they trot around the ring. Then, when a canter or lope is called for, all heck really breaks loose—draft horses are generally only worked at the walk and trot. I've actually had to run and hide to avoid being trampled by an errant draft horse attempting some semblance of a three-beat gait.

I've attended open shows where I have had the pleasure of judging Thoroughbreds, Morgans, Bashkir Curlies, Icelandic Ponies, and Mules all in the same ring. Simultaneously, some of these equines were ridden hunter seat, stock seat, saddle seat, and sidesaddle in both pleasure and equitation.

Open shows provide a judge with a great opportunity to examine and evaluate different breeds and disciplines. In chapter 3 we'll discuss how you can sort them out.

SCHOOLING SHOWS

Schooling shows provide a starting place for many show riders, as well as many horse show judges. Most schooling shows are put on and managed by individual stables to give their lesson students an introduction to showing. If you are judging a schooling show, you can expect to see many varieties of Beginner, Novice, and Leadline classes.

Some schooling shows are referred to as closed shows, which means that entries are open only to riders and boarders at the stable that is hosting the show. Open schooling shows welcome riders from neighboring barns.

At many schooling shows, judges are encouraged to give feedback to the riders. This is helpful for many young equestrians and beginner riders. Very often, these riders won't know they are doing something wrong unless you tell them. Beyond schooling shows, however, it is inappropriate to discuss performance with the competitors. There are two reasons: the time constraints of the show (every time you speak with someone, you are slowing down the show), and the appearance of impropriety or favoritism in speaking with only certain riders.

Schooling shows provide a great opportunity for a beginner judge to rack up some judging experience. Most schooling show managers

A rider dressed casually for a schooling show

will also be a bit more lenient on a beginner judge than an open show manager or recognized show manager would be. In fact, when you start judging, plan to officiate at lots of schooling shows. More to the point, they are often the only place an entry-level judge can begin his or her career.

INTERCOLLEGIATE SHOWS

The Intercollegiate Horse Shows (IHSA) encompass three major disciplines: Hunter Seat Equitation, Western Horsemanship, and Reining. Recently there has been some IHSA movement toward setting up a Dressage division, which I believe would be a great addition to the program.

I love judging Intercollegiate shows because of the strong emphasis on horsemanship and sportsmanship. Each show is run by a host college, which supplies the horses for all the competitors. Horses are randomly drawn and assigned to riders. The riders then have virtually no time to warm up with their designated mount.

When judging Intercollegiate shows, it is very important to remember that the majority of the riders have never sat on the horse they are riding before. In some ways a judge must work even harder to see through any horse problems that may affect the basics of good equitation that a rider is displaying. To me, it can be the purest form of horsemanship.

For instance, many riders tend to ride behind the motion on a strange horse as a defensive mechanism. They're sitting back because they're not sure what the horse is going to do, which in many ways is the safe technique. If sitting behind the motion interferes with the rider's performance, however, you must penalize it, as in a Hunter Seat Equitation class over fences. A rider who is behind the motion can easily get "left behind" over a jump, which is a serious penalty.

An Intercollegiate judge must remember that the horses being used will probably be ridden all day; there are not enough animals for everybody to have his or her own mount. Hence, you might see the same horse in six or more classes.

When I'm judging at an Intercollegiate show, I try to run each class as quickly and efficiently as possible. This way the horses have only to perform the minimum of work for the classes in which they are entered. You just can't expect these horses to canter or lope for as many times around the ring as you would expect in a recognized show—they would be physically exhausted.

Many rules at Intercollegiate shows are different from those at USAE or AQHA shows. One of the biggest differences is in Hunter Seat Equitation Over Fences. At an IHSA show, riders on course are not penalized for changing a lead with a simple change rather than a flying change. At a regular USAE or AQHA show, this would be heavily penalized. Also, an equestrian may be granted a "re-ride" on a different horse if the judge and/or stewards feel the horse was totally inappropriate for the rider.

I've judged IHSA shows where I've been told, "Well, Applejack doesn't get his right lead ever, so please don't count it against the rider." The show manager will then either point out Applejack or tie a colored ribbon somewhere on the horse indicating that he is limited in his abilities. Thus, a rider who has drawn a "one-lead" horse is not penalized.

Among other minor differences between IHSA shows and other competitions, there are usually three or four stewards at an IHSA show, where a typical recognized show might have only one or two, depending on the size of the show (stewards ensure a level playing field for all competitors by enforcing the show rules and regulations). Additionally, IHSA stewards are generally not licensed as stewards. They are coaches of the attending teams that have been appointed as stewards for that competition.

The IHSA allows only licensed USA Equestrian judges to officiate at its shows, so unlicensed beginner judges need not apply. Still, Intercollegiate shows are worth seeing as a spectator for the learning experience. Once at the show, if you have any questions about an IHSA rule, do not hesitate to ask one of the numerous stewards or the show manager. After the show, you can visit the IHSA Web site (www.ihsa.com) for more information.

4-H SHOWS

Every state in this country has an active 4-H program for youngsters to learn about everything from cows to rabbits to horses. Judging 4-H horse shows can be quite different from officiating at recognized or open shows. Certain classes—such as 4-H Project or Fitting and Showing classes—are seen only at 4-H competitions.

At many 4-H shows a judging protocol known as the Danish system is used to rank the riders. Rather than awarding ribbons for first through sixth (the most common number of ribbons awarded in a class), each rider is evaluated on his or her own performance and given a ribbon. There are usually three categories of ribbons—blue, for superior performance; red, for an adequate to good performance; and white or green (depending on the 4-H club and region of the country), for participating and fulfilling the basic class requirements. Generally, everyone gets one of these ribbons unless he or she falls off or is excused from the ring for being out of control.

The purpose of the Danish system is to rank riders by individual standards of performance against themselves rather than ranking

A judge contemplates how a rider should be pinned

them against the other riders. I like using the Danish system, but I will admit it can be quite challenging. If you have a class of twenty riders, you must get a good look at each of them and award ribbons accordingly to all. That's harder than judging at a "regular" horse show where you only need to worry about finding your top six to eight riders and scoring them in order.

From a financial standpoint, most 4-H clubs cannot afford to pay the same fee scale that recognized or open horse shows can offer. It is up to you to decide whether it is worth your time and energy to judge all day for $150 or $200. I usually judge one or two 4-H shows a year, and consider my work a donation to this worthwhile program.

SHOWS FOR RIDERS WITH DISABILITIES

One of the most rewarding assignments is judging a show for riders with disabilities. Common divisions at these shows include Equitation, Obstacle, Dressage, Pole Bending, Relay, Showmanship, Costume, and Futures (which is similar to dressage in that certain maneuvers are required, and each rider is judged individually and scored). Within each of these divisions, classes are broken down further by the capabilities of the riders. The riders may show independently (with no aide), with one aide, or with a leader and sidewalkers.

When judging a show for riders with disabilities, you need to learn as much as possible about each rider you are judging, both abilities and disabilities. In this way you can weigh the performance of one rider against another. Many judges at these shows start out as volunteers to learn the procedures prior to actually judging.

To learn more about working with and judging riders with disabilities, contact North American Riding for the Handicapped (NARHA), National Disability Sports Alliance (NDSA), or USAE, which now has a Riders With Disabilities Committee. Contact numbers and addresses for these organizations appear in appendix B.

CHAPTER TWO

Getting Started

IN MY OPINION THE FOUR ORGANIZATIONS with the strongest and most stringent learner judging programs are USA Equestrian (USAE), the American Quarter Horse Association (AQHA), the American Paint Horse Association (APHA), and the National Reining Horse Association (NRHA). Obtaining your license from any of these organizations will assure you a certain level of education and status in the judging community.

If you are going to specialize in one discipline, such as Reining, you will need to follow the guidelines of that governing organization, in this case the NRHA. Many breed organizations, such as the AQHA and APHA, also license judges, and the requirements vary from group to group.

Although I had been judging unrecognized and schooling shows for years, the first license I obtained was from the American Donkey & Mule Society (ADMS) in 1990. In 1993 I was licensed in Hunters and Hunter Seat Equitation by USAE (formerly the American Horse Shows Association—AHSA). The journey to achieve my USAE license took three years of learner judging, attending clinics, and judging unrecognized and schooling shows as often as possible.

The first time I applied for my USAE license I was turned down, told I needed to obtain more experience. This is quite common; many judges are turned down on their first application, which also helps weed out people who are not willing to put more time and energy into their craft.

When I was turned down, I went back out on the road and learner judged—learning the ropes of judging by accompanying licensed judges to horse shows—with as many judges as would let me. Although I was disappointed not to be granted my license the first time I applied, it was actually a blessing in disguise. I got to sit with so many incredible horsemen and judges that I was much better prepared as a judge.

Those interested in judging can also get a lot out of several judging programs available for students in 4-H, the American Quarter Horse Youth Association (AQHYA), and a few college-level judging programs around the country. Members of 4-H, the AQHYA, and some colleges participate as individuals and on teams in judging competitions. These programs are a great way to get started in judging and learn the ropes.

These programs, however, do not assure anyone of being granted a judging license from any specific organization. You will still have to fulfill the requirements of the USAE, AQHA, or the organization of which you wish to become a licensed judge.

The best route to being licensed by the USAE, AQHA, APHA, or NRHA is often to earn a "smaller" license first. "If your region has an organization that licenses judges, like the New England Horsemen's Council, go for that license first," suggests USAE judge Kim Ablon-Whitney. "Judging local-rated shows is a step up, and you will get to practice your skills with better-quality horses and riders, and hopefully get to judge some small regional medal classes."

Over the years I've asked various judges how they got started in the business. One of my favorite answers came from Arthur Hawkins, considered one of the top judges in the United States. He has judged many of the biggest Hunter/Jumper shows in this country, including The National Horse Show, the Washington D.C. International, and the Pennsylvania National Horse Show, and has traveled around the world to officiate. In a quiet moment at the Garden State Horse Show (the largest Hunter/Jumper show in New Jersey) some years ago, I asked him how and why he began judging.

Hawkins was brutally honest. "I had gone as far as I could as a rider, and was actually afraid to jump and show further. But I still wanted to be around horses and make my life with horses. Judging was the perfect answer for me."

For some great officials, judging careers grew out of their riding careers. For others, judging evolved from general equine and horse-manship skills. Both types of judges have a lot to teach you.

MOCK JUDGING

A good first step on your road to judging is to attend small shows and sit on the sidelines for the entire day. Try to evaluate each entry you observe, and keep track of your preferences. Do not skip any classes or take long breaks. Use the bathroom only when the real judge does. If you find your attention wandering or are unable to sit still for long periods, you need to decide whether you have the patience for judging.

USAE Registered judge and AHSA (now USAE) National Hunter Seat Medal Finals winner Rita Timpanaro suggests "practice, practice, practice! Practice judging as often as possible on your own and compare your results to the judge's when the class is pinned. Do this at local, C, B, and A shows."

Mock (practice) judging will introduce you to the all-important skill of bookkeeping, a necessary skill all judges must learn. It is one thing to have an opinion; when you are judging, you must also keep track of your opinions in a manner that makes sense to you and allows you to decide the winners in each class. Judging symbols in chapter 3 will help you begin mock judging.

After mock judging at a couple of small shows, it is time to contact the Licensed Officials Department of your chosen organization. Request the judge's enrollment package, which includes the current roster of licensed judges, the clinic schedule for aspiring officials, training programs, and learner judge application forms. The organization will supply further information on judging clinics and requirements.

Although most Hunter/Jumper people choose to become licensed with the USAE, and many Western horsemen align themselves with the AQHA, APHA, or NRHA, there are many other options available. Many different breed organizations (see appendix B) license judges. It is up to you to decide which organization will be the best fit for your talents.

LEARNER JUDGING

To begin the process of learner judging for the USAE, you need to apply just to receive your basic learner judging card. This is a prerequisite before you can even think about applying for your Recorded judge's license (known as a "little r"). The learner judging

SURVIVAL TIPS FOR JUDGES

Being well prepared will ensure that your day of judging will go much more smoothly. Look over these lists and add any personal items that you find necessary.

YOU MAY WANT TO BRING:

- Your own chair
- A pillow
- A change of clothes and shoes—in case you get muddy or slobbered on
- Hat or visor
- Umbrella
- A blanket
- Snacks, food, hard candy, and mints
- Water
- Sunscreen
- Chapstick
- Handi-Wipes
- A book
- Prescription medication (if appropriate)
- Raincoat
- Checkbook and credit cards
- Cell phone for emergencies—not for chatting with friends!

ALWAYS BRING:

- Rule book of whichever organization the show is affiliated with
- Your organization's membership card
- Your licensed official's card
- Stopwatch
- Whistle
- Pen
- Pencils—pens often don't write in the rain
- Wite-Out
- Clipboard
- Extra judge's cards—just in case the show manager has forgotten (judge's cards may be purchased from horse show supply companies that sell ribbons, trophies, and rider's numbers)

card, which allows you to pursue fulfilling your learner judging requirements, can be considered a "prelicense" for learner judging. The USAE's Licensed Officials Department will supply the Learner Judging Application Form upon request.

After that, the USAE, AQHA, APHA, and NRHA rule books list the learner judging requirements in order to apply for your license. For instance, if you are applying for your USAE Hunter license, you must complete six full days of learner judging at two shows (or more) while sitting with at least two Registered (known as "big R") judges. Additionally, you must learner judge a minimum of two A-rated Conformation Hunter divisions, although you can substitute a Hunter Breeding division or attendance at a Hunter Breeding clinic for one of the Conformation divisions. This must all be accomplished within a three-year period prior to applying for your "little r" Recorded license.

It can be hard work finding A shows that actually hold Conformation Hunter divisions. Very often, the division does not fill, so show management will cancel it. Plus, most Hunter/Jumper horse-

Remember to bring along a wide-brimmed hat when judging. On a hot, sunny day, a hat can make a huge difference in your comfort by reducing the possibility of sunburn and heatstroke.

men don't pursue getting only their Hunter license, so there is time to be spent on fulfilling the requirements for a Hunter Seat Equitation license, too.

To show how the requirements can vary from division to division, if you're applying for your USAE Western and Stock Seat Equitation licenses, you'll have to learner judge at least three recognized competitions with three different judges. This learner judging must be accomplished within two years prior to applying for your "r" license. Likewise, the USAE requirements are different for Andalusians/Lusitanos, Arabians, Hackneys, Driving, National Show Horse, Saddlebreds, Welsh Ponies, and other divisions. You need to read the rule book to find the minimum requirements for your chosen licenses.

It is wise to attempt going beyond the minimum listed requirements as you try to obtain your license. If the rule book recommends learner judging six shows, double that amount and learner judge at twelve. Better yet, go for twenty; no experience is ever wasted.

Each organization has a specified number of days prior to a competition in which they need to receive your learner judging application. For instance, the USAE must receive your application and fee at least twenty-one days prior to each show. This means you need to contact the show management and judge(s) for permission at least two months in advance. It is important to complete the required paperwork in a timely fashion.

Some shows and judges do not care to host learner judges, so be prepared for some shows to say no. I once called a horse show in New Jersey to ask whether I could learner judge. I ended up speaking with the show manager's wife, who was also the comanager of the show. I explained to her that I had already received permission from the judge I wanted to sit with. She thought it sounded fine. So

AN OPINION FROM JUDY RICHTER

When asked for her advice for beginner judges, legendary horsewoman Judy Richter offered pertinent and important thoughts in her typical no-nonsense style.

"My advice to a beginner judge is to judge *all* day long, for *many* days (at least ten), with a variety of judges whom he or she respects as a good judge. To be a good judge, you must first be knowledgeable, and second, learn a system to record your opinion (always remember the exhibitors are paying for *your* opinion).

"Judging with competent judges will enable you to devise your own system by taking the best of their bookkeeping systems. Experiencing long days of judging is also important; maybe it is not for you. Some people just cannot concentrate for twelve to sixteen hours at a stretch.

"Judging is not as easy as everyone thinks it is. Reading books about it may help—it can't hurt anyway. Expertise and a good bookkeeping system are what make a good judge, in my opinion."

I happily sent off to the horse show the paperwork that would give me official permission to learner judge at their show.

Within a week the husband (the other comanager) called me and told me he did not like learner judges (actually, he screamed it at me) and that I was not allowed at his show. I meekly mentioned that his wife had said it was okay. He said that it was not.

Meanwhile, because I had counted on doing this show, I had not contacted another show or judge for that weekend. Not having a show to learner judge put me behind in my plans. That's why I must advise you to expect such things to happen.

Whether you sit with USAE Registered ("R") judges or Recorded ("r") judges depends on your breed and discipline choice and the licensing organization. In order for your learner judging to count for credit, check the rule book to see which officials you are permitted to sit with.

It is also useful to learner judge at unrecognized or schooling shows. Although you will not receive official credit for these shows, you will gain valuable experience and perhaps another reference from someone willing to vouch for your competence on your licensed officials application.

Check around with other horsemen and judges for their recommendations on good judges to sit with. Some judges are notoriously antagonistic to learner judges. I know—I've sat with my share. One judge scolded me all day because he didn't like my bookkeeping system. He kept leaning over my clipboard saying things like, "That wasn't a late change of lead" while I tried try to explain that my judging symbol actually meant a rough change of lead. The bottom line was that he felt the only good bookkeeping system was his own; everyone else's was wrong. To say I had a miserable day would be generous.

One judge I sat with was wonderful, not because we agreed on placings, but because she could respect my opinion. I honestly couldn't tell what she was looking for a lot of the time in a winning round, so I flat out asked her. Although she and I didn't agree a lot of the time, we could see each other's points of view. And, after all, that is what judging—and, for that matter, life—is all about.

Another judge was very forgetful and didn't have a solid book-keeping system. Throughout the day, she kept saying things like, "I think I missed a couple of horses." Because a learner judge is not supposed to be the one doing the actual placings, this put me in a difficult position. I ended up making broad hints to this woman, who has since retired from judging.

No matter whom you are sitting with or where you are judging, dress neatly and conservatively. Men should wear a suit or sport coat and a tie. Women should plan on wearing a dress or a suitable pantsuit. Footwear depends on the weather and footing. I tend to wear paddock boots to shows where I know I will be spending a lot of time inside the arena near the horses. Then if I am stepped on, my toes have a fighting chance.

Women, do not, under any circumstances, wear shorts, jeans, mini skirts, or excessive makeup. You need to present a professional appearance, because you are representing your organization. I've worked a few times with one judge (who shall remain nameless) who always seems to push the horse show fashion envelope. When judging with her, I always find myself distracted by her outfits and makeup. I can't imagine what the competitors think. Remember, horse showing is a conservative sport, so dress conservatively.

Also remember to respect the privilege of representing your organization as a learner judge. Always promote a professional and pleasant image in your words and deeds. You, too, are being judged. I just can't emphasize this enough. Your whole focus should be on learner judging. Do not bring a dog along, and do not spend time hanging out with your friends.

Plan to arrive at the competition at least half an hour early. Once on the show grounds, report directly to the show steward or technical delegate. Give him or her your name, address, organization membership number, and present your learner judging card.

Check with each judge you work with as to his or her preference in answering your questions. Some officials do not mind if you ask questions during the class, while others prefer to wait until the class is over. Although your opinions will not count toward the official placing, many judges want to know how you scored the competi-

AMY THEURKAUF'S TEN COMMANDMENTS FOR LEARNER JUDGES

Amy Theurkauf, who recently received her USAE Recorded license in Hunters and Hunter Seat Equitation, is an active competitor in the Amateur Owner Hunter division with her horse, Remarkable. As per USAE rules, Amy is allowed to judge and maintain her amateur status because her full-time profession is a writer and tutor.

1. Arrive early—a minimum of half an hour before the first class.
2. Prepare yourself to learner judge. Bring your own judging cards, a clipboard, extra pencils, pens and paper, and the rule book.
3. Plan for the weather. Always bring extra clothes for cold conditions, even on warm days, since you may be under the shade of a tent. Wear comfortable, attractive shoes that are suitable for the ring. Bring a hat for warmth or shade and sunscreen. Carry your lunch, water, and snacks. Consider bringing a blanket and a towel to wipe the early-morning dew off your chair.
4. Read the specifications of each class you will watch, and be sure you have a copy of the courses.
5. Learn the rules of the divisions you will be watching.
6. Log details for each round as if you were the judge. The judge may ask you about a detail he or she accidentally missed.
7. Be courteous and respectful of the judge. Do not ask questions while the judge is working. Assess his or her style of working and teaching before asking questions.
8. Take notes on what each judge says. Notice your own strengths and weaknesses as you practice judging each day.

> 9. Volunteer to sit for additional classes above your require-
>   ments and to stay until the end of the day. Do not social-
>   ize with trainers or exhibitors.
> 10. Send thank-you notes to the judges and the horse show
>   management.

tors. Take this opportunity to discuss any questions you may have. Do not, however, offer an opinion if it's not asked for.

It is hard work to judge a horse show, and even more difficult for a licensed judge who has a learner judge by his or her side. "Understand your role is to learn. To do that, you must be prepared," advises top international official Eric Straus. "Know the rules, keep your thoughts to yourself, and then ask the senior judge all the questions you have only when it is convenient for them to answer."

Do everything you can to make the day easier for the judges and other officials you work with. Offer to fetch them a cold drink on a hot day and a hot beverage in cold weather. Any judge who allows you to sit with him or her should have your respect and gratitude for the educational opportunity you are offered.

To accurately judge each class, you must develop two important skills. The first is a shorthand system or list of symbols for marking the judge's card. This method varies from judge to judge. Ask judges you work with how their systems evolved and what works best. Use whatever system makes sense and is comfortable for you. There are certain symbols that are used almost universally whether you are judging Hunter Seat, Stock Seat, or Saddle Seat, such as WL (wrong lead), WD (wrong diagonal), NS (not suitable), and TF (too forward or fast). We'll take a closer look at common judging symbols in chapter 3.

The second required judging skill is the ability to keep track of and score all entries. At any moment you need to be able to give the announcer a standby list of the top competitors. By the end of the class, you should be instantly able to give the results.

At the end of your day of learner judging, make sure to thank the judge, the steward, and the show management. If required, give the judge the organization evaluation form to assess your performance, along with a stamped and addressed return envelope. Keep your scorecards and go over them at home to improve your skills. Send thank-you notes to any official or member of the staff who helped you at the show. A little thoughtfulness goes a long way, and they will remember you next time.

Learner judge Lilli Bieler

Robert Mayberger

ONE LEARNER JUDGE'S STORY

After a twelve-year career in the equine products industry with such companies as Pet Ag., Vita-Flex, and W. F. Young, Lilli Bieler knew it was time for a change. "I had been successful in marketing, sales, and sales management, but I realized my ultimate desire was to work more hands-on with horses," Lilli explained. "Also important was to restructure a career for myself involving horses that would enable me to maintain my amateur status for competition purposes. Judging was something I could legally do as an amateur with USA Equestrian." [Note that the USAE permits judges to compete as amateurs as long as the other amateur requirements are fulfilled. However, some organizations, such as the AQHA and the APHA, do not allow judges to compete as amateurs.]

Lilli felt she had the necessary skills to learn to judge and decided to try. "I have always been that person who can sit by the show ring for hours watching and never get bored. My mind is naturally curious and analytical, and I am always invigorated to witness a horse or rider do something special. I have a passion for the spectacular Hunter and the talented rider, but also an appreciation for the long road it takes to perfect the ultimate ride." These skills coupled with a lifetime of riding and showing experiences from local to A-rated competition were what Lilli felt would make her a solid candidate for the USAE Learner Judge Program.

"I judged a few unrecognized shows to test the waters, and I was hooked. Shortly thereafter I applied to the Learner Judge Program and was thrilled to be accepted. And the more shows I judged, the more I realized all the other benefits from judging. It doesn't matter what level the show, I always learn something from someone—even if it's what *not* to do. Of course, learner judging with 'R' judges is a tremendous learning experience, from improving judging techniques to swapping horse stories to discussing industry topics and trading training techniques.

"Being involved in judging keeps one's finger on the pulse of the industry. But it is also rewarding to be able to give back to a sport that has given me so much over the years. As I continue judging with my Learner license, and hopefully when I earn my 'r' rating, I will judge a lot of smaller shows attended by many riders just beginning their careers. I would like to think that I have something positive to offer them, and I am rewarded to feel I am doing my part for the industry."

Lilli had one unfortunate experience while learner judging in 2001. She arranged to learner judge with an "R"-rated Hunter judge at a Long Island (New York) horse show. Unfortunately, the judge (we'll call her Ms. X) decided to cancel at the last minute and did not inform Lilli, who had driven seven hours to attend the show. The judge who replaced Ms. X did not have a Registered license (she was an "r"), so Lilli's time learner judging would not count for credit.

There were three other judges officiating at the show, two of whom were "r's" and one who was a "R." In order for her time to count, Lilli needed to sit with the "R" judge. Unfortunately, the "R" judge did not want to have a learner judge sit with her. Eventually, the two show stewards prevailed upon the "R" judge to accept Lilli as a learner judge.

The lesson to be learned from this fiasco is that you need to confirm and then reconfirm any learner judging plans you make. Ensure that the judge(s) you want to sit with will be available, and don't hesitate to call them several times again after the initial contact.

BE DISCREET

It should go without saying that a learner judge must be discreet. You must not discuss the horses and riders with anybody but the judge you are working with. Your actions also must be above reproach.

Pinto Horse Association, International Buckskin Horse Association, and New England Horsemen's Council judge Don M. Tobey had an experience with a learner judge that is worth mulling over.

Tobey explained that "shows in eastern Canada offered for many years a regionally popular class in which, as I recall, the horse was to be judged 50 percent as a pleasure/performance mount and 50 percent on conformation (an unusually high weighting for conformation). Officiating at one of these shows, I had a learner judge, an extremely capable horsewoman, working with me.

"At the end of one such 50–50 class with many appealing pleasure horses, I had penalized one horse because of what I judged to be a moderately severe front-leg fault, moving it down to third or fourth in recognition of the high percentage based on conformation. Because my learner judge hadn't noticed the severity of the leg problem, I asked her to look at it before the entries left the ring. She dutifully walked clear to the far end of the arena, looked pointedly at the front legs of that one horse, and then marched back to confer with me. The crowd of several hundred spectators was chuckling, the learner judge was embarrassed by the attention, and the horse's owner was furious.

"While I believed I had made a good decision in placing the horse where I did, there's no question that I was less than diplomatic in my handling of the interaction with the learner judge and in focusing attention on a single entry in the class. It's a mistake I've been careful not to repeat."

COSTS INVOLVED

The cost of obtaining enough experience for licensing varies. Factors to consider include travel, lodging, food, and learner judging and application fees. It will be easier and cheaper to get experience if you live in a region of the country where there are numerous shows, such as the areas around New York, Florida, or California. Even if you are an active trainer or riding instructor and it's difficult to find time to learner judge, though, it's still well worth the effort.

I estimate I spent about $4,000 between air travel, mileage, rental cars, hotels, food, learner judging fees, and other miscellaneous expenses when I was learner judging for the USAE from 1990 to 1993. For some people, it is hard to justify such an expense. But you must remember that any advanced education, whether college, cooking classes, or riding lessons, costs money.

It is up to you to decide whether the money and energy you put into obtaining your license is worth the trouble. Some people decide not to become licensed because of the cost and hassle factors, and are quite content just to judge schooling and unrecognized shows where licensing is not a requirement.

APPLYING FOR YOUR LICENSE

In order for your application to be processed and considered by the Licensed Officials Committee, questionnaires and/or references with regard to your learner judging must be returned to the licensing organization. These questionnaires and references are then reviewed to ascertain your general knowledge and readiness to judge. Depending on the breed and discipline and whenever possible, most should be from licensed judges, technical delegates, or members of organization committees. Again depending on the organization, questionnaires are usually sent out by the Licensed Officials Committee to references you have listed on your application. The majority of your references should be prominent horsemen, judges, and other show officials.

Your application will be much stronger if more than the minimum number of favorable questionnaires and recommendations are returned to the Licensed Officials Committee. The number of USAE questionnaires that need to be returned varies for each discipline and breed; for example, for a Welsh Pony license, at least ten recommendations are needed. Prospective Hunter judges need fifteen questionnaires, while in the Reining division at least three evaluation forms from NRHA judges must be submitted.

Since not everyone who receives a questionnaire will return it to the organization, plan to send in at least twenty-five to fifty names, and more if possible. It is also a good idea to send notes to everyone to remind them who you are and where you worked with them.

When you prepare your application for processing, type it so that it presents a professional appearance. Make sure you enclose the correct fees, and mail well in advance of the deadline for reviews. It is also a good idea to send it certified, return receipt requested.

Reasons for rejection can range from failing the written test in the Jumper division to not having enough experience in the Arabian division. If you are rejected on your first application, do not give up. Focus your energies on gaining more experience, and then reapply. In many cases two or three applications are required before acceptance. Ask questions, learn from your mistakes, and try harder.

HELPFUL HINTS TO GET HIRED

When the letter arrives from the Licensed Officials Committee confirming that you've been granted your judging card, you eagerly hang out your shingle, order business cards, and place an advertisement in a regional horse publication. Now you sit and wait for the judging opportunities to roll in. However, no one calls. You wait some more, but still no one contacts you. What did you do wrong?

In many instances it's not what you did wrong but the way shows are run and managed that's the problem. Shows are not obligated to hire you. Most show managers are reluctant to hire a newly licensed judge because they have no way of knowing what abilities he or she possesses.

All show managers who run recognized shows refer to a directory of licensed judges that lists the divisions an official is licensed to judge as well as the names of the shows he or she judged the previous year. When there are so many experienced, well-seasoned judges available, why should managers take a chance on you?

It is truly a "Catch 22" situation: In order to get judging jobs you need experience, and in order to get experience you need to judge. Therefore, take an aggressive approach to convince shows to hire you. You may also have to make some sacrifices. Offer to judge on a complimentary basis, or request that only your expenses be paid. Although this may be a financial hardship in some cases, consider it an investment in your continuing education.

In the meantime, show managements need to know that you are capable of doing a professional and astute job. Try to judge as many schooling shows as possible, so you can list them on your judging résumé. Continue to learner judge with well-known judges and get them to write you references. Attend clinics given by well-known trainers and riders, then network with other people who attend. Friendly connections are a very valuable tool to further your judging career.

Sometimes you just need to call horse show managers and make them aware that you're available. If they do not know you are out there, they can't hire you. Even if they have already hired judges for their show, volunteer to help the day of the show. Act as ringmaster or help with the secretarial work. Once show management becomes acquainted with you, they are more likely to hire you the next time they need a judge.

Often, having one license is not enough. Most judges diversify and obtain licenses in more than one division. Many have either another breed card or are licensed in another discipline. The more well rounded you are as a judge, the more useful you are to show managers. Many shows will offer classes in addition to the breed or discipline in which you specialize. Rather than hire multiple judges, it is easier for a show to hire one judge with all the pertinent licenses. If you are truly only interested in judging only one breed or discipline, you are limiting yourself as a judge and horseman.

If you are officiating at a large show and one of the other judges becomes ill or has to leave for another reason, show management will be very happy if you have the card to fill in for that judge. But—and this is very important—communicate with the show manager if you do not feel capable of judging specific divisions or classes. "If you are not confident judging certain classes, tell the management," advises Rita Timpanaro. "This will save both you and the show manager a lot of potential headaches."

Depending on the show, the secretary or manager will call you several months in advance to book you to officiate at the show. During this initial contact, make sure that you are very clear about how much you charge and other such details. Most show managers want to know up front what they will owe you, so be sure to state your daily fee, mileage, food, and lodging costs (if required).

Other show managers will send you a contract in which you will state your fees, and then you return the signed contract to the managers. Either way, make sure that both you and the show manager have an agreement as to how much your services as a judge will cost.

I used to be a bit lax about these issues until I ended up judging the show from hell in northeastern New Hampshire. I was asked to judge a show five hours from my home. Generally, if a show is more than three hours away, I ask for a hotel room to be provided to me the night before the show. This show manager was adamant that she ran a small horse show and could not afford one for me.

So, being a nice person, I agreed to drive halfway to the show and stay with friends in central New Hampshire the night before. I got up at a time that I thought was plenty early enough to get me to the show on time. Unfortunately, the show manager neglected to give me accurate directions. She did not tell me that there was a major detour on the highway near the show and, hence, I would have to come into the show from a back road.

I drove in circles for a while until several nice people steered me in the right direction. I pulled into the show fifteen minutes late and was greeted by a screaming show manager. Not a good start.

Then, when it came time for lunch, I innocently asked if they had lunch tickets for me to use or if I just gave my name at the snack booth to get my lunch (the two most common ways of feeding a judge). The show manager huffily informed me that I was making plenty of money, was late for the show, and didn't deserve my lunch to be paid for (the only time I have had this happen in more than three hundred horse shows).

Needless to say, I was not a happy camper. Now I always ensure that every detail, including lunch, is discussed and agreed upon prior to judging a show. In that way, I know what to expect.

By the way, in terms of making plenty of money at this show, I broke down my costs to the show manager at the end of the day so she could see I actually lost money judging her show.

This is how it looked on paper at the end of the day, since the show refused to pay for food, mileage, or tolls:

- Four meals—dinner, breakfast, lunch, and dinner (driving to the show, during the show, and driving home from the show)—added up to $35.50.
- 510 miles round trip at 32½ cents per mile (the going IRS rate at that time) came to $172.25.
- Tolls added up to $1.50.

My total expenses came to $209.25. The show paid me $250. I made $40.75 for judging in a dusty ring with a nasty manager. I had to take a day off from work to drive to this show, so I actually ended up losing money. Never again!

The worst part of this deal was that this was not a "small" horse show. It had more than a hundred entries in my ring alone, and the show made enough money to have easily covered my expenses. What can you learn from my ordeal? Get everything in writing and make sure you are properly compensated, unless you truly don't care whether you make money or not.

I am not trying to say all show managers are trying to take advantage of you as a judge. Rather, I am just attempting to ensure that you handle judging in the same fashion you would handle a business agreement. Be clear, be polite, and get it in writing!

SHOULD YOU ADVERTISE?

Advertising can be a useful way to get more judging jobs. To effectively market and advertise yourself, you must thoroughly understand your strong and weak points. If you are great at judging beginners, mention it in your ad. Should you specialize in judging one specific discipline, state it clearly. However, if you are weak in a part of your judging, do not claim to be capable in that area. For instance, if you are very experienced judging Western Pleasure but not Stock Seat Equitation, make that very clear. False advertising will lose you more jobs than you will get.

List some of the shows you have judged, so people will have an idea of your qualifications. Avoid bragging or advertising about success as a rider or trainer, which has no relevance to your talents as a judge.

If there are certain types of shows that you will not judge under any circumstances, make sure to put this in your ad. This will save show managers from calling you when you'll just be telling them no. Some judges will not judge schooling or 4-H shows, choosing only to officiate at recognized competitions.

The best results in advertising come from local or regional horse newspapers and magazines. It does not make sense to place ads in your hometown newspaper unless you live in a town that has many horse shows (such as Middleburg, Virginia). Make sure the ad clearly lists your name, address, telephone number, fax number, and e-mail address if you have one. It is not advisable to advertise your rates. Some shows may not call because they think you charge too much, and these may be ones you might consider judging for less money in exchange for the experience.

The time of year you advertise can have a bearing on response. Running an ad in the fall is not the best idea if you live in the northern United States, but might work well if you live in the South. The best time to advertise in most regions of the country is January, February, and March, when most shows are booking officials for the season.

TAKE A HARD LOOK AT YOURSELF

Self-examination is necessary to progress in your judging career, as well as life in general. If you have advertised your judging services, volunteered in other capacities at shows, and offered to judge without payment, but still cannot get any judging jobs, you need to take a hard look at yourself and your experience. Have you truly "paid your dues" and learned all you can?

Experience is a tough thing to gauge. Ask horsemen you respect for their opinions as to your qualifications and readiness to judge. If they have concerns about your experience, it is time to learner judge again. Choose judges with whom you have never learner judged before to expand your base of knowledge. You may have fulfilled the requirements for licensing, but that does not automatically make you an expert. Becoming a judge, like developing as a horseman, is a constant challenge.

Are you difficult to work with? Putting it simply, some people are not particularly nice to be around. If you have been rude and obstreperous as a competitor or trainer, your reputation will follow you. Getting a judging license does not make you a better person. Show managers will hesitate to hire you if they feel you will be difficult with them or rude to the competitors. If your personality has been less than stellar in the past, it is time to turn over a new leaf and develop a more positive outlook.

CHAPTER THREE

Keeping Track

THE TIME HAS COME when you're actually at a horse show and have to make some sense of what you're seeing. No matter what you're judging, whether Hunter Seat Equitation or Western Pleasure, you'll need to develop a shorthand and bookkeeping system to rank the competitors. You'll also need to have a strong idea which faults carry greater weight than others.

Although you may obtain a specific license, such as one for Hunters/Jumpers or Western Pleasure, you may one day find yourself in a ring at an unrecognized show surrounded with Saddle Seat riders on American Saddlebreds, Arabians, and Morgans. If you have received the prize list in advance, you'll at least have warning that you may be judging some classes where you do not have a lot of experience.

That's why the more you learn about all breeds and all disciplines, the better a judge and horseman you will be. As I've said before, no education or experience is ever wasted. If you truly want to only judge one specific discipline or breed, you are going to miss out on many wonderful learning—and income-producing—experiences.

JUDGING DIFFERENT DISCIPLINES AND BREEDS

When judging multiple breeds and disciplines in one ring, you need to have a basic understanding of what is considered proper and acceptable in each breed and discipline. Since there is no way that this book can possibly review every breed and discipline, you'll need to do a lot of studying on your own.

A confident rider in a Stock Seat Equitation class

A nice-looking pair in a Hunter Seat Equitation class

Clix Photography

I've spent years studying breeds that I may not personally care for, but I know I have to judge. And even with breeds I'm not especially interested in, I've found some splendid individuals that have taken my breath away. There is an old horseman's saying that is very true: "A good horse is never a bad color." Let me add to that and say a good horse is never a bad color or a bad breed, and a good rider is a good rider no matter what type of saddle he or she uses.

When I am judging multiple breeds or disciplines in one ring, I use what I call the 100 percent system. It allows me to judge each entry based on what would be considered perfect for that individual breed or discipline.

For instance, in a Conformation/Halter class, you might have the following six entries:

- American Quarter Horse
- Thoroughbred
- American Saddlebred
- Arabian
- Morgan
- Welsh Pony

You must decide among these entries without playing favorites. I love Thoroughbreds above all other horses. This does not mean, however, that a Thoroughbred will automatically win the class. Each horse must be looked at according to the breed ideals of perfection for that specific breed.

In this class I will assign points based on the ideal of 100 percent to each horse. Our American Quarter Horse is cow-hocked, has an offset front ankle, and does not display the qualities that are sought in a Quarter Horse. A score of 67 percent represents to me how far from the ideal 100 percent this horse is.

Our Thoroughbred has a clubfoot and a ewe-neck; he's also goose-rumped and post-legged. I assign him a score of 52 percent.

The American Saddlebred is pretty correct—he has a long, strong back, a beautiful face, and an overall feeling of quality. He scores 95 percent.

The Arabian is just beautiful with a dainty dished face and a very correct hind end. Unfortunately, both front legs are slightly crooked, but not terribly so. The Arabian scores 86 percent.

The Morgan looks as though he is thirty years old. He has a sway back and is gray around the muzzle. He is, however, very correct structurally and displays the prominent cresty "Justin Morgan neck" that is so prized in the breed. So although he is of good quality, his age has taken a little toll on his conformation. I decide to look through that and give him a score of 83 percent.

The Welsh Pony is obesely fat (a common problem in ponies), but very correct in most ways. He is a bit upright in the shoulder and stands slightly camped out. He gets a 74 percent.

The class is therefore pinned in this order:

1. American Saddlebred—95%
2. Arabian—86%
3. Morgan—83%
4. Welsh Pony—74%
5. Quarter Horse—67%
6. Thoroughbred—52%

By using the 100 percent system, you can break down and rank any type of class no matter how many breeds or disciplines you may be judging.

BASIC REQUIREMENTS OF EACH DISCIPLINE AND BREED

To understand the basic requirements of each breed, you're going to have to put in some study time—and the same applies to activity classes. What may be acceptable with a Saddle Seat Pleasure may not fly in a Hunter Pleasure. And also to complicate the issue, you have different breed standards for pleasure classes, so a Morgan Hunter Pleasure horse goes totally unlike an American Quarter Horse Hunter Pleasure horse or a Hunter Pleasure horse at a Hunter/Jumper show.

Later in this chapter, however, we'll take a look at keeping track of the most common rider and horse mistakes to get you started.

EQUITATION SYMBOLS

✓+ or GB–Good Basics	T/I–Toe In
✓ or AB–Average Basics	STL–Stirrup Too Long
✓– or WB–Weak Basics	STS–Stirrup Too Short
Stiff–Stiff Rider	RTL–Reins Too Long
WD–Wrong Diagonal	RTS–Reins Too Short
WL–Wrong Lead	Flat H–Flat Hands
2-H–Two-Handed the Reins	I-H-I–Spreads Hands Apart
LLL–Loose Lower Leg	BTM–Behind the Motion
LLF–Lower Leg Forward	LS–Lost Stirrup
LLB–Lower Leg Back	HH–High Hands
Open Knee–Open Knee	RH–Rough Hands
Calf–Overgrips with Calf	JA–Jumps Ahead
Bugs–Roaches	LB–Left Behind
Perch–Perched	OE–Opened Early
Shove–Shove Release	DS–Drops Shoulder
NR–No Release	Ducks–Ducks
DN Sit C/L–Does Not Sit at	Elbows–Elbows Out
Canter or Lope	Looks ↓–Looks Down
NP–No Plan	Stir-H–Stirrup Home
Heel–No Weight in Heel	Rail–Drops a Rail
Heel ↑–Toe Down/Heel Up	OOC–Out of Control
T/O–Toe Out	

Hallie McEvoy

Judging symbols used by Hallie McEvoy

Remember, it's usually easy to pick a winner. The hard part is deciding who gets the lower ribbons and why. It is crucial that you have a reason and justification for every placing, and the reasons why someone did not earn a ribbon. This is not that hard to do in a class of six, but it becomes very challenging when you are faced with twenty-six riders.

JUDGING SYMBOLS

As far as judging symbols go, use what makes sense to you. I've developed my bookkeeping system over the years using suggestions

HUNTER AND PLEASURE SYMBOLS

✓+ –Good Form

✓ –Average Form

✓ –Below Average Form

XC–Cross-Cantered

WL–Wrong Lead

4-B–Four Beats at the
  Canter/Lope

HH–High-Headed

LS–Lead Swap

DNUB–Does Not Use Back

DNUH/N–Does Not Use
  Head and Neck

TW–Twists

Dwells–Dwells

ROOTS–Roots

PC–Pace Changes

MPC–Major Pace Changes

PC↑–Pace Change Up

PC↓–Pace Change Down

NAH–Not a Hunter (a horse
  that is more suitable to be
  a jumper)

Rubs–Rubs

NT–Not Tight

OE–Opens Early

BTB–Below the Bit

OTB–Over the Bit

Lips–Plays with the Bit

Rush–Rushes

DIVE–Dives

HOF–Heavy on the Forehand

Splits–Splits Legs over Fences

3-L–Jumps Off Three Legs

⌐–Hangs Legs in Air

Broke–Broke Gait

≈–Rough Area

CH–Chipped

S–Short Spot

Q–Quiet Spot

< –Jumps to Left

> –Jumps to Right

LC–Late Change

RC–Rough Change

VOGR–Victim of a Good Ride
  (not a great horse, but rider
  made horse look good)

VOBR–Victim of a Bad Ride
  (nice horse but not shown
  well)

X–Refusal

2X–Second Refusal

EL–Third Refusal or
  Elimination

OC–Off Course

OOC–Out of Control

FWD–Flirts with Death (a
  dangerous fence for horse
  or rider)

OMG–Oh My God! (a scary
  fence)

from other judges and by making up phrases or symbols that give me an accurate representation of what I am seeing.

USAE Registered judge Randy Neumann says that beginner judges should "get bookkeeping and shorthand down to a science so that you can mark your card without thinking. It is your second language, enabling you to recall a trip from your notes to support your decision."

Randy also advises beginner Hunter and Hunter Seat Equitation judges to "watch more than you write! A 'gorgeous' card full of notes is worthless if you miss something while looking down to write. Watch an entire line and the end of the ring until you see the lead change before you glance down to write. And I always watch until they leave the ring. The round is not over after the last fence."

I wish I could give you a firm formula and standard deductions for every fault you will observe, but everything in riding is a matter of degrees. Is one rider's loose lower leg worse than another riding behind the motion? It depends on the severity of each fault. In most classes you will be confronted with an array of rider or horse faults. To decide the ranking of the competitors will depend (except in Jumper or Barrel Racing classes, where scores are objectively and numerically tallied) on your personal opinion of their individual faults.

For instance, with all other things being equal in an Equitation class, I'll pin someone with a slightly loose lower leg over someone else with rough hands. My justification for this is that a rider's rough hands will affect the horse far more than a loose lower leg will. Of course, a lower leg that is flailing back and forth on the horse's side is a different matter. Again, you must measure the degree of each fault and weigh it against the faults of the other competitors.

Small classes often offer true dilemmas. For instance, a judge will have to pick six ribbon winners out of a class of seven "Short-Stirrup" Hunters. The top five horses are easy to choose. Sixth place, however, is causing a bit of a quandary. One entry had a great round with the exception of trotting two steps around one corner, a severe fault. The other entry was too forward around the whole course, verging on out of control. What do you do?

There is no easy answer. A Short-Stirrup Hunter is supposed to be very quiet and in control, but is also required to canter the entire course without breaking. Once again, judging is a matter of degrees. If you feel that the Short-Stirrup Hunter that trotted two steps should get the sixth-place ribbon because he was the safer of the two choices, that would not be a wrong decision. If you felt that the other entry, the one extremely forward for the course, was acceptable, that would be a valid conclusion. The important point to remember is to have a reason for every placing and be able to justify your opinion.

Randy Neumann has an important point to make about this issue. "We are hired to judge and reward quality, which is a hard thing to teach someone who does not have the knowledge and experience to begin with. Too many judge 'on errors,' being scorekeepers rather than judging quality. Errors have to be weighed on the type of class (for instance, Pre-Green versus Working Hunters), as well as the overall caliber of the class. Sometimes a cross-canter can still win, depending on what you have to choose from. In other words, do not reward poor or dangerous jumping over a quality horse with errors that did not scare you."

Nothing in judging is black and white. Everything must be seen in a series of positive and negative degrees. Your goal is to pick the best overall rider or horse at that time in that ring. You can't consider how certain riders rode the last time you judged them or that their trainer standing at the gate is someone famous. What is being judged is the exhibitor's performance at that moment in that ring right now. You can't judge on what might have been or who they are. You have to judge based on the performance in front of you.

THE NUMERICAL SYSTEM

Many judges use a numerical system to rank competitors in Equitation, Hunter, and Pleasure classes. Each judge has his or her own breakdown for errors and mistakes, but in the long run, it really doesn't matter how you score each fault as long as you are *consistent.* You need to apply the same set of scoring guidelines to each performance you witness. Nothing upsets competitors more than feeling that a judge changes his or her likes and dislikes with every class, or with every rider. Decide on a scoring system that works for you and stick with it.

Dave Johnson, who has been licensed with the USAE since 1969, uses a numerical system for judging. "The beginning judge needs to be quite careful in separating out the participants for pinning. That is, the beginning judge, while perhaps having a thorough background in the horse sports, must quickly pick out the winners; not always so easy.

"The beginner judge must start sorting out the good and not so good immediately, since he or she does not want to call for the final lineup without having a clear-cut order of placing. In other words, the judge must not wait until the final horse is in the ring to start to 'judge.'

"Having systems in place that quickly pick out who beats whom is imperative; I use comparative numerical 'cheat sheets'—a spare pad of paper—after determining many years ago that there just wasn't enough room to keep accurate track of the current standings

A ROUGH GUIDE TO SCORING

The following is a rough guide to how I score riders and horses. Remember, this is only my guideline; use whatever works for you and makes sense for your style of judging.

90%+	An excellent performance.
80–89%	A good to very good performance.
70–79%	An adequate to good performance with a few mistakes.
60–69%	A less-than-average performance with significant mistakes such as wrong leads or cross-canters.
50–59%	A poor performance that might include losing a stirrup, breaking to a trot on a Hunter or Hunter Seat Equitation course, or two-handing the reins in Western and Stock Seat Equitation.
Less than 50%	Major errors including jumping or obstacle refusals.

on the average score sheets. These sheets also quickly enable me to provide a number score, and pin the class to the announcer as the last horse is leaving the ring."

A numerical system of judging also makes it easier for competitors to understand your judging. For instance, if a rider asks you to explain your placings, it is very simple to state that he or she achieved a 75 percent behind two riders who had a 78 percent and an 84 percent. You can then add why the rider scored a 75 percent without giving details of the other riders' performances. Remember, the only performance you should discuss with a rider is his or her own.

THE RIDER'S APPEARANCE

I am constantly asked whether a rider's appearance and clothing should be evaluated. At recognized and breed shows, there is a certain standard that must be adhered to. For example, riding in a T-shirt is not acceptable.

But at unrecognized shows almost anything often goes as far as clothing is concerned. I don't like it, but sometimes you have no choice but to pin a rider wearing a T-shirt. Here's why:

Say, for instance, we're judging a class of Low Hunters Over Fences with six entries.

Entry 1: A young Thoroughbred ridden by a local professional. The horse is well turned out and braided; the rider is polished. They enter the ring but it turns out they're only there to school. They have four good fences, but the horse gets quick, so the professional circles once before the next fence, a technical refusal. Everything else goes okay.

Entry 2: An ancient 14-hand pony with a rider who is about six feet tall. The pony trucks around the course very well . . . but a tall rider on a 14-hand pony is *not* suitable.

Entry 3: An adult rider on a horse that jumps in a very unorthodox style. He hangs, twists, dwells, splits, leaves out strides, has major pace changes, and is just plain dangerous. The horse and rider make it around without going off course, but the horse is not what you would call a hunter by any stretch of the imagination. (My symbol for this type of round is OMG, which stands for "Oh My God!")

Entry 4: A tiny child on a 16.3-hand Warmblood, which trots on the corners. This pairing is just as unsuitable as the six-foot rider on the 14-hand pony.

Entry 5: A teenager on some kind of a horse—you can't tell because they are going so fast they look like a blur. The speed increases through the round . . . they've now hit Mach 3 and managed to get two strides in a four-stride combination. And because they are trying so hard, they also manage to cross-canter.

Entry 6: The rider in the T-shirt with dusty breeches, rubber boots, and a green schooling helmet. Well, they may not look great, but the horse trucks around at an even pace, jumps evenly, gets his changes, and—best of all—is truly safe. The rider, although she doesn't look the part, does a solid crest release and stays out of the horse's way, allowing the horse to show off his talents.

Okay, time's up! The announcer needs the results—whom did you pin?

Although the rider is not turned out as well as I'd like to see, Entry 6 wins. Why? Because it is a Hunter class and I'm supposed to be judging the horse, not the rider. Although I wish the rider were dressed more appropriately, at least the horse got the job done. Everyone else had major faults. And remember, this was not a recognized show. If it were, someone would have hopefully loaned Entry 6 a ratcatcher, jacket, and velvet ASTM helmet.

This little exercise was just to give you an idea of what you will be confronted with a lot of the time. You can't let the rider's clothing obscure your search for the best horse or rider.

DOES WEIGHT MATTER?

As with the issue of clothing, a rider's weight can be the cause for great debate. Some officials will never pin a rider they feel is overweight no matter how good a rider he or she is. I don't think this is fair.

As a judge, you may have to look through the shape of the rider to see his or her horsemanship. In all honesty, I've seen very heavy equestrians who ride "lighter" on horses than some very slender equestrians who have rough seats and heavy hands.

Adverse rider weight is a hard thing to measure. A slimmer figure most often does look better than a heavier body on a horse. That being said, if I don't feel that the horse is struggling with the rider's weight, and the rider's weight is not negatively affecting his or her performance, the rider should be judged just like any other rider.

DOES TACK MATTER?

When asked whether nice tack makes a difference to me as a judge, I would shout an emphatic "no." Unless the tack obviously does not fit the rider or the horse, I am not looking at the tack in a performance or equitation class—I'm looking at the horse or rider. Although I'd like to see every Western rider in a beautiful Dale Chavez pleasure saddle and every Hunter Seat rider in an elegant Arc de Triomphe saddle, not everyone can afford this superb equipment.

As long as the tack fits and is clean and functional, it is suitable. A judge should not spend an inordinate amount of time staring at the tack; that time could be better spent focusing on the horse and rider's performance.

HUNTER SEAT AND STOCK SEAT EQUITATION

Whether they ride Hunter Seat or Stock Seat, most riders begin their show ring career riding equitation. Equitation, sometimes known as horsemanship, is judged on the rider's position and control of the horse.

Hunter Seat Equitation is a far cry from the old-fashioned hunt style of riding from which it evolved. The open galloping of fox-hunting has given way to a more controlled and refined show ring performance. Stock Seat Equitation is also much different from the type of western riding you see on ranches or in such rodeo competitions as Barrel Racing or Calf Roping. In both cases equitation has been elevated to the status of art.

There is no way I can review every type of position or equitation rider you will see. Once again, you'll have to put in study time and a lot of learner judging to train your eye to catch the various subtleties of equitation. Overall, the most important detail to evaluate in equitation riders is their positions. A rider should have good basics (marked as GB on my card) at the halt, walk, trot/jog, and canter/lope. Beyond that basic requirement, a host of other details must be judged, such as the rider's control of the horse and the soft or harsh quality of the rider's hands.

A competitor's ring savvy is a factor, since good competitors know how to hide their faults. Riders who are ring savvy will know when to show themselves off to you and also when to hide. For instance, riders with lovely posting trots should ensure that you see them many times at the trot either by circling or cutting across the

Julie McClain on Joe Bubbles Star demonstrates good basic Stock Seat position. In the next photos, Julie will show deviations from the ideal Stock Seat position.

ring through your field of vision. These same riders may go "hide" at the canter behind other horses so you can't scrutinize their canter position closely. This is smart and savvy riding.

When judging Hunter Seat Equitation on the flat, diagonals (the practice of posting the trot up when the horse's outside shoulder is forward) and leads (the horse's inside legs must precede the outside ones at the canter) are crucial elements in evaluating the competitor's performance. In "beginner walk-trot only" classes, diagonals are frequently missed by the riders. Ideally, a rider should be able to "feel" his or her diagonals, but most beginners need to look to see if they are on the correct one. This leads to the common fault of looking down that many beginner riders demonstrate.

In walk-trot-canter Hunter Seat Equitation, both diagonals and leads count toward the final placings. Even though it is the horse that picks up the lead, it is considered the rider's responsibility to

Lower leg back

Lower leg forward

Riding with the toe in removes the calf from the correct position.

Riding with the toe out opens the knee angle excessively.

Kim Asher on Calvin shows good basic Hunter Seat equitation, although her hands are slightly forward. In the next photos, Kim will demonstrate deviations from the ideal Hunter Seat position.

Lower leg back

Lower leg forward with toe and knee turned out

Hallie McEvoy

The rider is roaching (rounding) her back.

Hallie McEvoy

Hands too high

The rider's hands are flat, and her arms are straight and stiff.

ask the horse for the correct one. As with beginner riders looking for the diagonal, many novices look down to find their leads until they learn to do it by feel.

If you are confronted with two otherwise equal riders, a wrong diagonal is worse than a wrong lead. This is because a wrong diagonal is a more fundamental mistake. It is even within a beginner rider's capabilities, and should be penalized more heavily than a wrong lead.

A common mistake for beginner Stock Seat Equitation riders is "two-handing" the reins. Unless a Stock Seat rider is riding a young horse in a snaffle or a bosal, he or she must steer and control the horse with one hand; either the left or the right is permissible. Two-handing the reins occurs when the rider uses both hands on the reins either to obtain more control over the horse or, in many cases, because he or she is nervous. It is considered a major fault.

Another frequent problem in both Hunter Seat and Stock Seat Equitation that beginner riders display is breaking, or slipping from

Catherine Knight Photography

Judge Lauri Foster takes note of an equitation rider looking down.

one gait downward or upward into another. Breaking from the canter/lope to trot/jog or the trot/jog to walk must be penalized. The class requirements call for performing a gait when it is asked for; any deviation from this will move a rider down in the placings.

Losing a stirrup is also a major fault. Even if competitors ride well without stirrups, unless you've asked them to drop their stirrups, they should be penalized.

No matter how wonderful a rider is in one direction of the ring, anyone who rides poorly in the other direction should not receive a ribbon. There are, however, many exceptions to this rule. If you have six people in a class and all six people make major mistakes, you're going to have to pick the "best of the worst." This happens more often than most people can imagine. When I am confronted with such a class, I try to pick the winner based on who has the best overall position and control of the horse.

At times I have been confronted with a class where five otherwise good riders made major mistakes. The only rider to ride cleanly might have been a competitor with only average basics, a weak rider. He or she may not be the best rider in the ring, but for the purposes of judging he or she is the winner. Why? Because this

A Stock Seat rider using a bosal, which requires two hands on the reins

is the only rider who filled the basic class requirements of walking, trotting/jogging, and cantering/loping in both directions without any major faults.

EQUITATION OVER FENCES

Hunter Seat Equitation classes over fences bring a new host of standards to obtain that prized blue ribbon. First, the basic class requirements must be fulfilled—the fences must be ridden in the correct order, the course must be taken at the canter (unless it is a beginner class and trotting is allowed), there should be no refusals, and the rider and horse should meet each fence at the appropriate takeoff spot. The competitor must also jump in balance with his or her horse, not getting "left behind." Along with these requirements, the rider should display proper equitation position both on the flat and over the fences.

When judging Equitation Over Fences:

1. A rider who has a refusal should never pin above a rider with no refusals.
2. A competitor who is left behind should not pin above a rider who has "gone with" the horse over every fence.
3. A rider who loses a stirrup should not pin above someone who has kept his or her stirrups during the whole round.
4. A brief cross-canter is preferable to a wrong lead or a trot-change, because a cross-canter indicates that an effort was at least made to correct the problem.

A good example of a rider getting left behind

Dolly van Zaane Photography

A rider who has totally lost her position. Her lower leg has come too far back, and she is hanging on her horse's mouth with her hands.

Judge Timothy Cleary watches as an equitation rider roaches his back and jumps ahead of his horse.

An equitation rider with a good, solid position in air. I would prefer the rider's mouth to be closed for the sake of her overall appearance.

What do you do if one rider gets left behind, another rider loses a stirrup, and there are only six people in the class (meaning everyone must receive a ribbon as long as he or she wasn't eliminated)? Again, it depends now on the degree of each fault. I will pin someone who briefly lost her stirrup above someone who was badly left behind on a fence. My reasoning is that the lost stirrup probably had a far less significant impact on the horse than the rider getting left behind and falling out of position.

HUNTER UNDER SADDLE, HUNTER PLEASURE, AND WESTERN PLEASURE CLASSES

Hunter Under Saddle and Hunter Pleasure classes are similar in that the horse, not the rider, is judged. The difference between them is that in a Hunter Under Saddle class, the most important attribute is the way the horse moves. In a Hunter Pleasure class, manners are of paramount importance. A Hunter Pleasure horse does not have to be the best mover in the world (although he should at least move evenly and be sound), but he must be mannerly and kind. A good mover is a plus. A Western Pleasure horse is judged on both movement and manners.

A Hunter Under Saddle is judged on performance and soundness, so the horse should move forward lightly, with a long and low stride. The horse must be balanced with a relaxed head and neck. In order to differentiate a good mover from a poor mover, you're going to have to spend a bit of time studying various horses. Don't be surprised if two people can't agree on whether or not a horse is a good mover; often two judges can't even agree.

Faults in a Hunter Under Saddle class include wrong leads, pace changes, a high head, playing with the bit, stiffness, high-stepping with excessive knee action, and being heavy on the forehand. Additionally, such way-of-going faults as winging or overreaching must be noted and penalized.

A Hunter Pleasure horse should look as though he is enjoying his job. Ears should be pricked forward, and gait and pace should be even. Although manners and willingness are the two most important attributes of a Hunter Pleasure horse, a good mover is a definite bonus. Faults in a Hunter Pleasure class include pinned ears, spooking, jigging, and not standing quietly in the lineup.

A good Western Pleasure horse should have three even gaits: a balanced, flat-footed four-beat walk; a cadenced and easy two-beat jog; and a clean three-beat lope. Judges used to pin horses that were excessively slow and displayed a four-beat shuffle lope rather than a true three-beat lope. Now, however, most judges penalize a Western Pleasure horse that does not display clean gaits. The horse should go on a loose rein with light contact. Faults for a Western Pleasure horse include wrong leads, ear pinning, opening the mouth, swishing the tail, high-headedness, and poor manners.

Bonnie Miller holds seven judging licenses (AQHA, APHA, NRHA, Palomino Horse Breeders Association, Appaloosa Horse Club, Pinto Horse Association, and National Snaffle Bit Association) and has judged for more than twenty-five years. Some of the most prestigious shows in which she has officiated are the APHA World Show, the NRHA Futurity, the National Western, the Pinto Nationals, and the Fort Worth Stock Show. Bonnie is very definite as to what she wants to see in a winning Western Pleasure horse. "Whether I am judging Quarter Horses, Paints, Palominos, or Appaloosas, I am looking for a good mover that stays consistent without showing signs of intimidation. I like to reward excellence, and do not judge on the negatives. I try to let the best horse win. A Western Pleasure horse should move forward at all gaits and exhibit true, cadenced gaits. I prefer a horse that appears natural yet obedient to the rider's cues."

Bonnie's point about rewarding excellence and not judging on the negatives is very pertinent for all judging, not just in Western Pleasure. Earlier in this chapter, Randy Neumann also makes the point that judges are hired to judge and reward quality. Although you are looking out for faults, you don't want to miss anything that is wonderful or extraordinary. Don't become so hung up on mistakes that you miss the overall picture.

Any behavior that is considered dangerous, such as rearing or kicking, is cause for elimination, as is lameness. Martingales, tie-downs, bandages, and boots are forbidden in Under Saddle and Pleasure classes.

Suzy Lucine Photography

A lovely Morgan Hunter Pleasure horse—Kathleen Peeples and Cabot Top Attraction

A nice-moving Appaloosa Hunter Pleasure horse. Ideally, the horse's ears should be forward.

A high-stepping Amateur English Pleasure Morgan—Amy Gatewood riding Everreddy GSF

An American Quarter Horse in a Western Pleasure class

Clix Photography

A sharp-looking Morgan Western Pleasure horse—Dwayne Knowles with The Vintage Touch

You should also note that a Hunter Under Saddle at a Hunter/Jumper show goes very differently from a Morgan Hunter Under Saddle or an Arabian Hunter Under Saddle at a breed show. The same can be said for an American Quarter Horse or Paint Western Pleasure horse versus a Morgan Western Pleasure horse. You must study what each discipline and breed specifies in a Hunter or Pleasure horse.

HUNTER OVER FENCES

Hunters have evolved in quite a new direction over the past few decades. Thirty years ago outside courses over hills were quite common, with long approaches to most fences. Obstacles more closely simulated fences found in the hunting field, such as stone walls and coops. Boldness and a good forward speed were rewarded. Now most Hunter Over Fences classes take place in perfectly level rings with exact striding specified. A more uniform and slower pace with even and quiet jumping are required.

As with a Hunter Seat Equitation Over Fences, certain class requirements must be met to be in the ribbons. The course of fences

ADVICE ON RUNNING YOUR UNDER SADDLE CLASSES

Veteran hunter and jumper judge Randy Neumann has some great advice to share about Under Saddle classes.

He recommends that you "run your Under Saddle classes quickly and efficiently. The longer you hack them, [the more likely you are to] lose your winner, and it looks like you can't decide among entries. Try to choose those in contention for a prize during the first direction. Then watch those during the second direction as to where you really think they belong in the order."

must be ridden in the correct order at the canter without refusals. The horse should meet each fence in a consistent manner. Additionally, striding should match what the course designer had in mind—a four-stride line had better be ridden as a four-stride line.

I may be a bit more lenient in this regard than other judges. If a horse is short-strided but a wonderful jumper, I'm not going to heavily penalize him for putting an extra stride in a long line if it looks right for that horse. Not every horse is gifted with a huge stride, and if you judge only on striding, you're going to inadvertently eliminate a lot of gifted horses.

A good Hunter Over Fences should jump with even knees reaching toward his chin. Legs should be tucked tightly below the knees. The horse must use his neck and back in an athletic manner. Common faults for a Hunter Over Fences include rubbing (touching the fences), hanging (dangling lower legs in air), rushing (or hurrying) fences, missing a lead change, bucking, knocking down fences, and refusals.

SHOWMANSHIP AND FITTING AND SHOWING

Many open and breed shows, as well as 4-H shows, feature Showmanship or Fitting and Showing classes. Both classes are judged with the horse being led in-hand. Stock Seat horses are shown in a halter and lead rope or shank. Hunter Seat and English horses are presented in a bridle and bit. Handlers should be dressed in their show clothes, and the horse should be well groomed and sparkling clean.

Showmanship is judged strictly on how well the handler shows off the horse to the judge. When at a halt, the handler should never place him- or herself between the judge and the horse, but rather should "display" the horse to you at all times. There are certain ways of holding and leading the horse. The two methods most favored are the quarter system and the half system. The quarter method is used mostly by advanced competitors, while many beginners favor the half system.

In the quarter system, the competitor moves with the judge staying a quarter of the horse away from the judge. Imagine splitting the horse into four quarters:

- Left front (near) section
- Left hind section
- Right front (off) section
- Right hind section

When the judge approaches the horse at the left front shoulder, the handler should move him- or herself to the right front section of the horse, one-quarter of the horse away from the judge. Should the judge approach the horse's left hip, the handler would move to the front left section of the horse.

The half system divides the horse into right and left halves. If the judge approaches anywhere on the horse's left side, the handler should be on the right side. If the judge is on the horse's right side, the handler should move to the left side.

Any movements the handler makes should be smooth and quiet. The horse should be obedient and stand evenly. The judge may also request walking and trotting patterns to see how well the handler shows off the horse.

There are certain characteristics that good handlers share. They make frequent eye contact with the judge (also known as spotting), they carry themselves with good posture in a relaxed and crisp manner, and they always anticipate the judge's moves.

Two books written about Showmanship will help the aspiring judge. Both volumes, *Understanding Showmanship* and *The ABCs of Showmanship* (Alpine Publications), were written by Laurie Truskauskas. I highly recommend both as tools to assist in your Showmanship judging training.

Fitting and Showing varies just slightly from Showmanship. In Fitting and Showing the handler is being judged 50 percent for his or her showmanship abilities, with the other 50 percent based on the horse and rider's cleanliness and turnout. Fitting and Showing, which is very popular at the 4-H level, serves as a good introduction to more advanced Showmanship classes at breed and larger shows.

LEADLINE

Frequently, as a beginner judge, you may find yourself starting out by judging Leadline Equitation riders. Although this may seem simple at first glance, it can be tough. There is nothing worse than being surrounded by ten cute little riders on even cuter little ponies and having to award just one blue ribbon.

A very cute Leadline rider

Some shows make it easy for you as a judge by letting you give everyone a blue ribbon. Most shows, however, expect you to actually rank these sweet little tykes.

Many judges will rush through Leadline classes, considering them unimportant. I couldn't disagree more. Always remember that these are the riders of the future. If they are not encouraged in the show ring, they may take up baseball instead.

Over the years I've developed a few tests to see which Leadliners actually know what they are doing and which are just posed on the horse. Any of the following tests/questions (depending on the age of the Leadline rider) will help you pick a winner.

- What color is your horse?
- What breed is your horse?
- How old is your horse?
- Without looking down, could you drop your stirrups and then pick them up?
- Please lay your reins on the horse's neck and put your hands on your hips. Now, please pick up your reins.

I've had some hilarious answers to the question "What color is your horse?" One little girl thought long and hard before she replied, with some prodding, "Well, I think my pony is bay but my mother says he is green and he'll always be green!" I was still laughing three classes later.

I once asked a young boy on a striking Appaloosa what breed his horse was. He proudly announced that his horse was an "Apple Loser." These are the moments that make judging Leadline special for me.

I like using the rein test because it shows which children have actually been taught the basics, and which had the reins placed in their hands just before the class. This has become my standard Leadline "test" over the years, and it's definitely very useful as a tie-breaker.

When judging Leadline riders, just remember that you are still looking for the same attributes you would in a more advanced equitation rider. You want the riders to have good basics (heels down, eyes up, and quiet hands) and a good attitude (showing is fun). The hardest part for you as a judge will be separating cute riders from good riders.

Working with Other Show Officials

ALTHOUGH THE JUDGE is often the most visible official at a horse show, he or she is just one of the many needed to ensure that an event flows smoothly. As a judge, how you interact with the other officials and staff can have a direct bearing on how well the show runs.

STEWARDS AND TECHNICAL DELEGATES

Depending on the discipline you are involved in, you will either be dealing with a steward or technical delegate while officiating at a show. You'll usually work with stewards at Hunter/Jumper and Western shows, while technical delegates can be found in a similar capacity at dressage, three-day events, and combined driving competitions. Both stewards and technical delegates are charged with making sure that the competition adheres to the rules and regulations of the organization that has sanctioned the event.

Although some people think of stewards and technical delegates as "police officers" at a competition, I prefer to think of them as supportive experts who have a great knowledge of the rule book. They are there to ensure that the playing field is level for everyone and that the horses involved are treated in a humane manner.

To me, the steward is the most important person on the show grounds. And if you are an entry-level judge, a good steward can help you immensely with his or her knowledge of the rules and an even-handed way of dealing with conflict.

Sherry Robertson of Edgemont, Pennsylvania, has been a USAE steward for more than twenty-five years and is also licensed as a FEI

Hillary Strong judging an Open Jumper division

Catherine Knight Photography

(Fédération Equestre Internationale) chief steward. She has officiated at some of the most prestigious shows in the country including The National Horse Show, the American Gold Cup, the FEI Children's Jumper Championships, and Florida's Cosequin Winter Equestrian Festival.

Says Robertson, "My advice for entry-level judges is to read the rule book thoroughly . . . then read it again! Know the rule book well before ever judging a horse show. Read not only the parts concerning the divisions you want to judge, but also the basic rules and regulations of your organization. Be prepared!

"An entry-level judge who has a problem or question should ask to speak to the steward right away. Do not wait until a small problem turns into a big one. The judge should ask the manager or announcer to have the steward come see them, but do not have the request announced over the loudspeaker system. It should be made over the radio." Robertson believes it is better that the whole show grounds not be made aware that a judge and steward are going to meet and speak; the judge and steward should meet quietly and privately without competitors and spectators trying to hear what is going on. For instance, if there is a question as to whether a piece of equipment a rider is using is "legal," the judge and steward can share thoughts and consult the rule book to formulate a decision without alerting the competitor. If the equipment is legal, then no one on the grounds, including the rider, will know a question has arisen. Should the decision be that the equipment is not legal, the steward can then quietly inform the competitor.

When Robertson is called in to handle a conflict, she says she "listens very carefully to all parties, and I always try to find a quiet place to discuss the question or problem. The in-gate or the horse show office are usually *not* the place to have the discussion due to the number of people in those locations. I allow only the concerned parties to take part. I like to discuss the problem separately with each individual before bringing them together.

"Staying calm and polite is very important, although it is not always easy in difficult circumstances. I also ensure the show manager is aware of any potential problems, and I always keep the other stewards working at the show involved in any question or problem as it evolves."

Robertson also feels it is important to educate judges and competitors when conflict arises. "I will show the concerned parties the parts of the rule book that apply to the question or problem. If I am unsure of how to answer a question or problem, I know I can call the USEA to discuss the problem and get an answer." The USAE has someone available around the clock and on weekends to handle any issues or concerns a steward may encounter.

Early in her stewarding career, Robertson received some important advice from legendary steward Iris McNeil, who officiated at almost every major show during her career. "I was lucky to work with Iris several times early in my stewarding career. The best advice she gave me was, 'Never carry your rule book with you!' The few minutes it will take you to walk to the office or your car to retrieve it will give you time to collect your thoughts and find the proper rule without an irate person looking over your shoulder."

Stewards like Robertson make it much easier for a beginner judge to focus on judging, rather than worrying excessively about the rules and difficult competitors. Never be afraid to ask questions of the steward, whether it be to clarify a confusing rule or to see how he or she handles conflict. Also, if the show is short-staffed and there is no one to get you a drink or food, many stewards are happy to bring you sustenance since you often cannot leave the judges' stand. If you learn to work with show stewards rather than regard them with suspicion, your career as a judge will go much more smoothly.

Should you find yourself working with an indifferent steward, you'll have to make some decisions for yourself. One steward I've worked with spends the entire day in her car reading rather than touring the show grounds. If I approach her about a concern, she'll tell me to handle it as I see fit—not exactly an ideal answer. The last time this happened, I went right to the show management and told them I was not receiving the support and assistance I required from the steward. The show management had a chat with the steward, and then the steward came to see me. Although she was a tad bit grumpy that I had "told" on her, she did make an effort to offer me assistance.

Luckily, this type of steward is the exception rather than the rule. I've been privileged to work with several particularly talented and affable individuals through the years, such as Jackie Martin, Bev Bedard, and Kathy Kennett, who are supportive and anticipate problems.

RINGMASTERS

Depending on the breed or discipline you are judging and/or the size of the horse show, you might work with a ringmaster. The ringmaster is the person who will assist you by directing the competitors while they are in the arena. The ringmaster will either shout directions to the riders or will call the announcer via a walkie-talkie to have the announcer give the directions. Your ringmaster will also be responsible for such problems as an out-of-control horse or a fallen rider. Getting along with your ringmaster is crucial, as this is the person with whom you will have the most contact throughout the day.

However, if you know that there will be a horse that is showing signs of being wild, you as a judge can plan proactively. I always have a plan that I discuss with the ringmaster and/or the gate keeper should a horse bolt off in the ring. Sometimes it's as simple as running for cover while having the rest of the class halt. At other times I will have the ringmaster focus on the "problem" horse or rider the entire time he is in the ring so that the ringmaster can anticipate a problem I might not see because I am looking at the other riders.

One problem I have encountered with ringmasters is that they sometimes overstep their duties and try to judge a class with you. I've had ringmasters tell me, "Number 94 is bucking, number 15 is on the wrong lead, and number 132 has broken from the lope to the jog." This may seem like a help, but do not use any information you are given unless you see it with your own eyes. If you personally didn't see something happen, it didn't happen.

The reason for this is simple: The information the ringmaster may be so helpfully providing could be wrong. It also looks very un-

Judge Timothy Cleary hands his results to the ringmaster.

Catherine Knight Photography

professional to the competitors that the ringmaster, rather than the judge, is pinning the class. The riders are paying you, the judge, for your opinion of their talent, not the ringmaster's.

I instruct my ringmasters to notify me only of the following three situations:

1. If someone is out of control and about to run me over, I want to know.
2. If someone has fallen off and I haven't seen it yet, the ringmaster should ask all riders to halt.
3. If someone behind me is on the wrong lead, the ring-master can quietly say to me, "You might want to turn around now."

Any further information is too much information.

This is, however, not to say that you can't make small talk with the ringmaster and have a laugh or two. There are some shows I look forward to because of the ringmaster I will be working with.

Ninety-nine percent of the time your ringmaster is a volunteer. I've worked with ringmasters who in "real life" were surgeons, golf pros ("my wife dragged me here"), scientists, hardware store managers, models, and corporate CEOs. It's one of the reasons I love horse shows—you meet some very interesting people.

GATE KEEPERS

Most judges will agree with me that the gate keeper of your ring (also known as a starter) is a crucial key to the show's organization. Why? Because he or she is the one person who can make the biggest difference in how long the show runs.

A great gate person will rapidly get horses in the ring for the class and then quickly get them to leave the ring after the class. A good gate keeper will get the competitors lined up and ready to go in the ring promptly. On the other hand, if no one has been assigned to wrangle the competitors and open and close the gate, the show will become disorganized very quickly.

So learn your gate keeper's name and buy him or her a cold drink. If you've got a happy and organized gate keeper, I guarantee your day will go better than you can imagine.

PADDOCK MASTERS AND SCHOOLING AREA SUPERVISORS

The paddock master or schooling area supervisor is the person who watches the schooling area to ensure safety. Although most judges do not have much contact with the schooling area supervisor, always make a point of saying hi and introducing yourself. I've had schooling supervisors tip me off beforehand to keep an extra eye on an out-of-control horse or a very frightened rider. These types of tips can make a huge difference in how you run a class.

COURSE DESIGNERS AND TRAIL DESIGNERS

Whether you are judging at Hunter/Jumper or Western shows, you will work with a course designer or trail designer. At a Hunter/Jumper show the course designer will lay out the Over Fences courses for Equitation, Hunters, and Jumpers.

The course designer posts the courses outside the ring for the riders, and also gives copies to the judge. Always inspect the courses yourself to ensure that the striding is set correctly and that the course looks safe, such as ground rails all in place, extra jump cups removed from the jump standards, and no litter in the ring that might trip or spook a horse. Communicate freely and openly with the course designer about any concerns involving the fences, the distances, or the footing.

It is also important that the course you are holding in your hand is the same one as the course that is posted outside the ring. I learned this tidbit the hard way. I once judged a show in which the first rider entered the ring and proceeded to jump a different course from the one I was given. I called the rider off course and dismissed her from the ring. The next two riders did the same thing—they jumped the wrong course.

At this point I thought I might be going crazy, so I walked over to where the courses were posted only to discover that the diagrams the course designer gave me were not the same ones she had posted. Needless to say, I had to give re-rides to the three riders I had eliminated. I was rather embarrassed about the whole situation, which could have been avoided if I had checked my courses against the courses that were posted.

Trail course designers create trail courses for beginners through advanced riders. As a judge, you are usually much closer physically to the trail course when judging than you would be to a course over fences. Hence, it is easier to see the course and go over the design you have been given to ensure accuracy.

JUMP CREW

Members of the jump crew are traditionally the least appreciated workers at a Hunter/Jumper show, yet they probably work harder than anyone else. They unload the jumps from the trucks, set up the courses under the direction of the course designer, change the heights and distances of the jumps throughout the show day, and rebuild any fence that is knocked down. And then they have to put everything away. So much work for so little money!

A few people actually make their living being professional jump crew members. I don't know if I could do it given the physical labor involved and the lack of respect they get from the average show rider.

When you are judging a Hunter Over Fences, a Hunter Seat Equitation Over Fences, or a Jumper class, your jump crew is a very important part of keeping your ring running smoothly. Jump crews responsible for multiple rings are kept running among them.

The jump crew can't be everywhere at once, so don't get mad at them if they're trying their best. Instead, fix fences yourself when you can, or ask trainers standing by the in-gate to put fences back up. Most trainers are only too happy to help, since it cuts down on the length of the show.

As with your gate keeper, treat your jump crew well. Buy them drinks and snacks. Inquire after their well-being. You may find that if you are nice to the jump crew, they will hang around your ring more than the other rings that are running. This will make less work for you.

Emergency Medical Technicians (EMTs)

Emergency medical technicians (EMTs) are hired by show management to respond to any accidents on the show grounds and attend to the injured parties. Their presence is mandatory at USAE-recognized horse shows.

Often the only person to have fully seen an accident is the judge. Your input can be invaluable to the EMTs when they are treating the victim. If you've seen the rider land on his or her head or back, tell the EMT. Often the injured person is not capable of explaining what happened, so your information about what occurred can be invaluable to both the EMT and the accident victim.

Since we live in a litigious society, if I've witnessed a serious accident, I make notes about it. You never know when you will get a call from either a lawyer or an insurance company asking what you saw that day. It is a lot easier to describe what you saw if you have made notes.

One important detail that is often overlooked is to inform the EMT when you arrive on the show grounds about any medical conditions of your own that could require treatment during the course of the show. For instance, because I am allergic to bee stings, I always carry a bee sting kit with me. I tell the EMT where I keep my kit in case I am stung and can't get to it myself.

Announcers

A good announcer is a blessing, because he or she will help keep the overall show—not just your ring—moving along, constantly informing folks about what class is going on in which ring and giving other pertinent information. The announcer will let people on the show grounds know if a horse is loose, if an in-gate needs to be cleared because it has gotten too crowded, or if a class is about to close (that is, about to start being judged).

The announcer at some shows will also "call the class" by announcing which gaits are required in classes on the flat, and "pin the class," or announce the winners. Other shows have the individual ringmasters of each ring do this job. Much depends on the size of the show; in a large show, your ringmaster will be the likely person to call and pin the class for you.

The announcer may also be in charge of the walkie-talkies and will assign different radio frequencies to each ring. Be very circumspect when speaking on a walkie-talkie—you never know who might be listening. If you call the announcer while his microphone is open, you may impart information to the whole show grounds that you would rather no one know. At one show, for instance, when a horse trotted into the ring, an unleashed dog also entered the arena. Not realizing that his microphone was on and that the announcer's mike was open, the judge commented to the person sitting beside him, "Aw lawd, now we got *two* dogs in the ring!"

When working with an announcer, always double-check when you call your results in. "If you mix up your cards, or mix up the numbers when you call in the results, fix it," states USAE judge Ann Jamieson. She also points out that you should "listen to the announcer, and make sure you got it right, and he got it right. Don't ever be afraid to say, 'Oops, I misread the numbers, here's the correct order.'"

MANAGERS

The majority of show managers I've worked with through the years have been wonderful people who care about judges' comfort during the show. They make sure that you have good directions to the grounds, that you are fed, and that you have a decent place to stay if you are coming from a long distance. I've even had show managers ask me if I preferred the Hilton to Holiday Inn. Once when I judged in Louisiana, I was offered a choice of jambalaya, crawfish ("crawdaddies"), or shrimp for lunch. As a judge, it doesn't get much better than that.

Once your contract, requirements, and fees for judging have been established and you're at the show judging, there is a lot you can do to work with the show management and make their life easier.

As has been said earlier but bears repeating, always arrive at the horse show at least thirty minutes early. Once you are on the show grounds, it gives the manager one less thing to worry about; nothing is worse than wondering where all your judges are and whether they will arrive in time. On the grounds, check in with the manager and/or secretary, collect your clipboard and courses (if required), and head to your ring.

At the ring, don't wait for the manager to introduce you to the show staff you will be working with. Making the introductions yourself will help get the show on the road. If the trail or jumping course isn't ready, pitch in and help build it. Remember, even if you haven't set the course, the course is still the ultimate responsibility of the judge. Check to see that the fences for Hunter Seat classes are set at the correct distances or that the trail course is ready to be ridden.

If you are having a problem working with one member of the staff, bring it promptly to the attention of the show manager. Although this would seem to be the commonsense approach, it is amazing how many judges just complain rather than deal with an uncomfortable situation. If you don't bring an issue to the show management's attention, they can't be expected to read your mind.

The show manager wants the day to run smoothly for competitors, the staff, and the licensed officials. Anything you can do to ensure a successful outcome will be remembered with gratitude.

SECRETARIES

Like the show manager, a show secretary will be hard at work on a show for weeks in advance and for days afterward. In addition to keeping track of exhibitor numbers, class entries, and payments, the secretary is often also required to stay in contact with the judges throughout the day regarding entries for each individual class.

I will often radio in to the secretary prior to a class or a division to ask how many competitors I am expecting if the gate keeper does not have this information. As a judge, it is nice to know if you're waiting for five or twenty-five riders, and whether there are any late additions to a class.

The secretary is responsible after the show for filing the show results with the organization that the show is affiliated with and for closing the books on a show. Sometimes the secretary will have to chase for months after competitors who either neglected to pay or bounced a check.

One of my favorite secretaries is Virginia Rice from Huntington, New York. Virginia always contacts me at least five months in advance of a show to book me, she sends me a contract to fill out with all my pertinent information, and she inquires after my health and my family. At the show, Virginia is friendly, helpful, and just an all-around pleasure to work with. She also makes sure that I am fed and, if it is sunny and hot, that I have an umbrella to sit under. After the show she asks if I have any suggestions or thoughts about the show. Virginia is the type of secretary who is wonderful to work for.

VOLUNTEERS

Volunteers will staff most of the shows that entry-level judges officiate. Some fund-raising shows for clubs or nonprofit organizations are managed, run, and staffed entirely by volunteers.

It is important to realize that you may be the only person on the grounds being paid for your services. Although many all-volunteer shows run just as well as professionally managed ones, you must be willing to overlook minor mistakes on the part of eager amateurs.

Often you will be paired with a ringmaster or gate keeper who has never been in that position before. Heck, they may never even have been near a horse before. This need not be a problem for you as an official. Just take the time to explain what you require from your volunteers, and 99 percent of the time they're happy to oblige.

Common Judging Situations and Problems

ONCE YOU'VE BEEN JUDGING FOR A WHILE, whether licensed or not, you'll run into certain recurring circumstances. Whether it is an unsafe horse-and-rider partnership, an irate parent, or a rustic bathroom in the woods at a show, each judge has his or her share of "war" stories.

"The universal conversation by officials is about strange situations and how to apply the rules," comments Eric Straus. "I've encountered this conversation at all levels, from the backyard horse show to the Olympic Trials and even to the Olympic Games. Judges want to make the right decision and they never stop testing themselves and each other. The conversation usually starts, 'What would you do if? . . .'"

"Even the best judges will tell you that so many things come up at shows that you will never have imagined or prepared for," shares Kim Ablon-Whitney. "You need to feel calm and confident to deal with them. Judging a million local and one-day shows won't necessarily prepare you for everything you'll see in the future, but it will prepare you to feel competent."

Randy Neumann reminds prospective judges that "just when you think you have seen and done it all—surprise!" There are always strange new judging experiences lurking around the next corner.

I've had some really bizarre things happen while I was judging, and I've felt foolish more than once. I once stepped into the ring to survey a typical Halter/Conformation class of Thoroughbreds, American Quarter Horses, and Warmbloods. There, peeking from the end of the line, was a Bashkir Curly, a horse I had only seen in magazines. The owner smiled at me. I beamed back to hide my panic. I had not realized that I would be judging a Bashkir Curly, and had not studied up on the breed.

Nevertheless, before me stood an actual Bashkir Curly in full dreadlocked splendor. I poked around in the hair and nodded enthusiastically. It pinned third in a class of twenty, causing the owner to thank me profusely for recognizing his horse's quality. If he only knew how petrified I had been. In order to evaluate this horse, a member of a breed I wasn't familiar with, I looked at his overall conformation—legs, chest, neck, and topline—and evaluated his quality based on the conformation of an average horse.

Another Conformation class consisted of Hunter ponies. As I walked down the line, a small mouth reached out and bit my derriere, which produced an embarrassing hole in my dress. As I rubbed my now very sore and pony-slobbered behind, the creature tried to bite me again. I fended it off by swatting it with my clipboard. Not a stellar moment for either the pony or me. The lesson learned from this situation? Be on your guard even around innocent-looking equines.

Once in a Hunter Over Fences class I judged an Icelandic Pony with the traditional bells and ribbons in his mane and tail. He proceeded at a merry, full-tilt "tolt" (a gait similar to a trot but with extra "beats") around the course, putting in some very unorthodox jumps. Every time he landed, all the bells would ring. A musical round, but not terribly Hunter-like.

At another show, a very pregnant woman insisted she ride in the Open Jumper division. Horse show management decided the insurance risk was too great and they forbade her to show. Her response was to sit and block the entrance to the ring for the other competitors. The progress of the show was halted for more than an hour as people pleaded with her to move. Friends later gave me a makeshift birthing kit in case I ever need it in my judging travels.

In yet another show, I was forced to explain that a Western Pleasure rider was using an illegal bit. The twelve-year-old rider was very understanding, but her grandfather was not. He stood on the rail the rest of the day and booed each of my decisions. Did I mention he stood about six foot five and weighed close to three hundred pounds? Unfortunately, the management of this unrecognized show was also intimidated by this fellow, so no one approached him about his unsuitable behavior. This was definitely a situation that should not have been allowed to continue throughout the show—and would not have if a steward had been present on the grounds—as it set a very poor example for the riders. I had the show manager escort me to my car at the end of the day, lest I run into this gentleman (and I use that term lightly) as I tried to leave.

Judging injuries are more common than you would think. I have had one too many a narrow escape from a wild rider headed directly at me. I routinely sunburn the tops of my hands and feet, despite the amount of sunblock (with numbers like 245) I use. Twice I have fallen out of the judges' stand. The first time it happened I had leaned on the rail to get a better look at an Under Saddle class. The plank gave way, causing me to perform a face plant into the path of an oncoming Trakhener. From my then horizontal perspective, the front end of that horse had an uncanny resemblance to a freight train.

On another occasion, I was viewing a flat class from the back of an elderly flatbed truck with nonexistent sides. As I leaned to watch a horse go by, another horse snapped at my face. Abruptly I leaned back—and flipped out of the truck. I landed directly in the ample supply of mud available at this show. My Laura Ashley dress ended up around my armpits, while my pride ended up in the next state.

Probably the strangest experiences I have had have occurred while trying to run to a bathroom between classes. I have gotten lost while on the way to a Porta-John "just over that hill" on more than one occasion. Competitors have followed me to the bathroom and carried on conversations with me as I have tried to relieve myself. One old-style wooden outhouse had a large sign inside that stated SPLINTERS CHEERFULLY REMOVED!

What I'm getting at here is that it is helpful to have a sense of humor. As I said in the introduction, although your role as a judge is not to be taken lightly, you need to keep everything in perspective. It is a heck of a lot easier just to laugh about some things than get upset about them. Just make sure that the competitors know you are not laughing at them, but rather at the absurd situation you find yourself in.

STAYING FOCUSED

Judging is hard work mentally, and it is important that you stay fresh and focused throughout the day. Taking a moment now and again to stand and stretch or change your position while sitting can redirect your energy and help you get through another hour of judging.

If you really have to go to the bathroom, make the time to do so. There is nothing worse than rushing through classes because your bladder is about to explode.

Judge Lauri Foster observes Short-Stirrup riders.

Catherine Knight Photography

If you are judging consecutive flat classes, you may find yourself standing for long periods of time. Comfortable shoes or boots will make a huge difference in how your legs and feet feel at the end of the day. I tend to favor Ariat paddock boots for the ankle support they provide and the cushy insole that keeps my feet happy.

To stay alert, I compulsively eat mints and cinnamon Altoids while judging. For some reason, the bursts of flavor enable me to stay chipper and focused. Each judge has favorite snacks and foods that keep him or her going. I know one judge who eats licorice all day long and another who eats mini chocolate doughnuts. And there are a lot of judges addicted to coffee and diet sodas. The bottom line is to do whatever it takes to keep your mind clear and focused on the job at hand.

TAKING CHARGE OF "YOUR" RING

Even if you have a ringmaster supervising your arena, you as the judge have the ultimate responsibility for what goes on in "your" ring. If a horse is out of control, you need to make the decision to dismiss that horse from the ring. Although the ringmaster may be the one to give the rider the news, the decision must come from you.

You are also the one who has the ultimate authority as to how long you will wait for riders to enter the arena. If the show manager has not put a "hold" on a class to wait for a trainer or rider, it is up to you as the judge to decide how long you will wait for an individual.

Often, riders lag outside the in-gate despite the gate keeper asking them to enter the ring. When this happens too frequently, I ask the steward (at a recognized show) or the manager (at an unrecognized show) to put a "clock on the gate," which means to set a time frame in which riders must enter the ring. If riders do not enter the ring within that time, the judge then has the discretion to eliminate them from the class. If you as a judge have been kept waiting five minutes or more, I believe it is totally reasonable to give a rider anywhere from 60 to 120 seconds to get into the ring.

It is important to remember, however, these pertinent words from judge Randy Neumann: "You are hired to judge, not to manage the show. If management elects to wait for exhibitors, do not complain."

Another common problem, especially in beginner classes at unrecognized shows, is trainers who go into the ring between classes to confer with their riders. I don't mind this as long as the visits are brief. When the conference lasts too long and the trainer has been warned to leave the arena by the ringmaster and the trainer isn't budging, I'll sometimes just start the class. That usually gets people moving in a hurry. Once again, I don't mind trainers coaching their riders in a brief fashion, but when they hold up the show and the other riders, something needs to be done. If everyone is aware and considerate, this is not a problem. But human nature being what it is, sometimes you as the judge must make the decision to move things along. Should a trainer continue to stay in the ring, the rider should be eliminated from the class.

Often, in Over Fences classes, riders who have been eliminated for too many refusals will ask to jump a courtesy fence, an easy fence to give both horse and rider back their confidence. Depending on the rules of the organization that the show is affiliated with (some divisions and organizations do not allow courtesy fences for riders once eliminated), the judge may have that discretion.

I have very mixed feelings on this issue. If a rider has had three refusals, that is elimination by the rules. Should you as the judge take up the other competitors' time by allowing the eliminated rider to "school" over a courtesy fence? In my book, you should do this only if it is allowed by the rules of the organization. And if you have any doubts about the ability of the rider and/or horse to jump the courtesy fence safely, say no.

What then happens if you give permission and the horse refuses the courtesy fence? Do you allow them to keep trying until they get over it? No—one try and then they must exit the ring. A horse show is not a time to school unless you are at a schooling show that permits such action. Remember, it's called a horse *show,* not a clinic or training session.

How you manage and run your ring will have a lot to do with the overall flow of the show and how many hours the show will run. Be organized, take charge, make decisions, and move things along when necessary.

STRESSING SAFETY

The most important thing you do as a judge, other than actually judging classes, is to ensure that safety is a priority in your ring. If you sense a dangerous situation evolving, do something about it. Do not wait until something happens to take action.

Once while I was judging, a pony rider entered the ring for a class, picked up a canter, and bolted out of the ring. The trainer caught the rider and pony five feet outside the gate and dragged them back into the arena. I immediately dismissed them on two grounds:

1. A rider who has entered the arena for a class may not leave the ring without the prior permission of the judge. Leaving without permission is elimination.
2. It was obvious to me as a judge and horseman that the pair would not be able to steer and stay in control. For that reason alone, a judge can eliminate a competitor.

The trainer and the rider's mother were not very happy, but judges aren't there for a popularity contest.

Similarly, a horse may become out of control in the ring, most frequently at the canter or lope. When this happens, I ask the class to halt until this rider resumes some semblance of control. Then I will ask them to leave the arena for their own safety and for the well-being of the other competitors in the ring.

Along with watching for out-of-control horses, be mindful of horses that kick or attack others in any way. Most responsible show riders will put a red ribbon in the tail of a kicker; the signal tells other competitors to steer far away from this horse. Unfortunately, however, some horses will find a way to kick other horses even when they are nowhere near one another. On more than one occasion I've seen a horse stop dead in his tracks and fly backward across the ring to kick another horse—if only they could be that athletic in their show performance. I never hesitate to request that such a horse immediately leave the ring. I don't like to give second chances when injury can be the result.

Beginner riders often have steering issues that require judges to make tough decisions. Riders who cannot steer and stop their horse successfully and are impeding other competitors create a safety issue. In this case, especially with young riders, I'll have the ringmaster hold the horse still in the center of the ring while I judge everyone else. Then I'll talk with the rider about ways to improve control. I always try to be very encouraging and upbeat because beginner riders can be very sensitive. You want a rider to leave the ring feeling that the experience was worthwhile even if things didn't go his or her way.

Beginner riders often do not deal well with unexpected changes in the show ring. Judge Don M. Tobey had an experience that is worth sharing. Tobey related that "good show judging is, even for the most expert and experienced judge, a learning process. And one way to learn is from our mistakes: recognizing them, then working to improve in the future.

"Judging a beginner walk-trot equitation class in a New England show several years ago, I asked the class to enter the ring clockwise, rather than the usual counterclockwise direction. This routine is legal under most rules, but also unusual, and it is something I occasionally ask of more experienced riders. For this beginner class, it was a near disaster. Riders who had prepared diligently and who no doubt already were tense and nervous became confused and never pulled themselves together as the class went on. I immediately concluded that requiring that reversed routine was an error, and I have never since asked it of a beginner group. While a rider at any level should 'expect the unexpected,' we judges need to be aware of what is and isn't reasonable to ask of riders and horses."

BANNED EQUIPMENT

It is very important that you understand which pieces of equipment are allowed or prohibited in particular classes and divisions. Equipment to look out for includes martingales/tie-downs, bits, leg wraps, and horse boots.

In 99 percent of classes on the flat, martingales and tie-downs are not allowed. There are a few exceptions to this rule, one being certain phases of advanced Hunter Seat Equitation "USET" type classes and another at therapeutic horse shows, where a rider is sometimes allowed to use a martingale for safety reasons. In all other cases, though, martingales and tie-downs are not permitted in classes on the flat.

Since there are literally hundreds, if not thousands, of bits that riders may choose to use, you need to do your homework and study the rule book for those that are allowed and under what circumstances they may be used. For instance, a three-year-old American Quarter Horse in a Futurity class will be eliminated if he's in a long shank bit rather than a snaffle. A gag bit is not permitted in Hunter classes, but may be used in the Jumper ring.

Leg wraps and protective horse boots are allowed in some classes but not others. An Equitation horse over fences or a Jumper may be shown in leg wraps, while a Hunter may not. Run-down boots and bandages are common in Reining classes, but forbidden in Western Pleasure classes.

If you have any questions on legal equipment issues, do not hesitate to ask the steward.

AVOIDING FAVORITISM/CONFLICTS OF INTEREST

When a person has an interest in a transaction substantial enough that it does or might reasonably affect his or her independent judgment in acts he or she performs for another, it is a conflict of interest.

—*Vincent Barry,* Moral Issues in Business, *1994*

A frequent topic of conversation for both judges and exhibitors is the sticky subject of conflict of interest. Many judges train horses and riders in addition to officiating at horse shows. This can cause problems when a judge is asked to work at a horse show in which his or her students would normally compete.

Most organizations forbid officials to judge someone with whom they train or have a current business relationship. However, if a judge waits a specified number of days or months (depending on the organization), he or she may then judge former students and business partners. Unfortunately, most trainers cannot afford to take months away from training, and riders seldom want to skip shows so their trainer can judge. Hence, many judges do not maintain an active training or coaching schedule.

Another issue under the heading of conflicts of interest is common at shows: Although the judge may not have active business relationships with the competitors, he or she may have long-term friendships with some of them. Is this fair to the other competitors? It depends on the judge.

When I am judging at a horse show where friends are riding, I work extra hard to maintain a professional distance from them. Any friends also know that they have to ride twice as well as everyone else to receive a ribbon. Is this fair to them? No, but it is the only way I feel comfortable and know that I will not be accused of impropriety.

"Be very careful fraternizing with exhibitors," states horse show manager and judge Jane Dow. "Usually, you do know some of the participants. Acknowledge them, but don't allow them or yourself to be too casual or chummy. Although innocent, it may be misconstrued by others."

The role of a judge is to be an impartial observer. If you are thinking about a horse you sold to a certain competitor, how much better someone's riding is since he or she switched to training with a buddy of yours, or whether a horse is for sale, you're going to get into trouble. If these factors influence your judging, you have let politics creep into your officiating, and you will be less effective (and possibly less popular) as a judge.

Judge Ann Jamieson puts it very succinctly. "Always judge what is right in front of you in a particular class. It doesn't matter what the horse or rider have done before, whether it was in the class before, or even if you're judging last year's Equitation finalist winner or Horse of the Year in the Green Hunters. Every class is a new start. Every horse or rider deserves the same chance.

"Don't ever let anyone intimidate you. Again, it doesn't matter who it is. If a top trainer is standing inside the gate so you know whose kid, or horse, it is, it doesn't matter. Just ignore it."

Judge Dave Johnson adds that "the old saying 'to thine own self be true' is so valid. The judge must never be swayed by famous exhibitors or an aggressive management. Consistency is always the name of the game."

There is no way I can review every situation you may encounter that might be construed as a conflict of interest; nor can I be your moral compass. You must look into your heart and decide the correct path.

COPING WITH CONFLICT

Try as you might to avoid it, at some point you will encounter conflict of other kinds. Every judge has stories of disagreements with competitors or other show officials. This is the nature of a sport that is judged based largely on opinion. How you handle conflict will make the difference between your being a happy or miserable judge.

Rule 1 of Judging: There is one winner in each class and a bunch of also-rans. That translates to making one person very happy with other people in varying degrees of satisfaction or dissatisfaction.

Rule 2 of Judging: Whatever happens, it is always the judge's fault. Never mind that the rider fell off and the horse jumped out of the ring; the chaos is somehow your doing.

If you can accept Rules 1 and 2, you are well on your way to being an emotionally well-adjusted judge. Still, you will encounter conflict, which comes in many forms.

Lame horses, or horses that are perceived as lame (depending on whom you speak with) cause more than a fair share of conflict. A horse that may be serviceably sound for a beginner Equitation class might be too lame for a Western Pleasure or Hunter Under Saddle. Why the difference? Equitation is judged on the rider, and as long as the horse is serviceably sound (stiff or with just a slight favoring of one leg) and comfortable doing his job, the rider can be fairly evaluated. Once you enter the Western Pleasure or Hunter Under Saddle ring, however, a different set of requirements apply. One of the things you are judging on in those classes is the soundness and evenness of the horse.

Once at a small horse show, a horse jogged around in a beginner Stock Seat Equitation class in a way that I felt was a bit more than stiff, but still acceptable for his little rider at the walk and jog. In other words, I felt the horse was serviceably sound for his job. The horse, unfortunately, showed up later in the day with a different rider in the Open Western Pleasure. The horse for the purposes of that class was lame, so I dismissed the entry. Pretty soon I had the show manager and an irate parent wanting to discuss this issue. The whole time I spoke with them I was very careful to say things like "in my opinion" rather than just state that the horse was lame.

I needed to explain why the horse was acceptable in one class (a beginner Equitation judged on the rider) and not in another (a Western Pleasure judged partly on soundness). I spoke softly and slowly, and explained my position as best I could, rather than getting angry in return at them. My attitude helped defuse the situation and allowed the parent to calm down and learn something about horse showing.

At another memorable show, an angry father confronted me because I had not awarded his daughter a ribbon in any of her classes. (This was at an unrecognized show, so there was no steward to run interference.) Because these were Hunter Seat Equitation classes, diagonals and leads counted toward the final placings. This young rider could not find her diagonals and could not get her horse to canter on the correct lead. Six other riders managed to put in good showings and earn ribbons.

It turned out in speaking with the father that he had no idea what diagonals and leads were, nor did he know how important they were. Once I quietly explained the requirements of the classes, he calmed down, apologized, and left me alone.

I will not tolerate horse abuse of any kind. Randy Neumann agrees. "Do not tolerate or reward abuse or temper tantrums in your ring. Training should be done at home, not in the show ring."

When I'm judging, a rider who overuses the whip or draws blood with spurs will be dismissed from the ring. I'm pleased to report that over the past three hundred or so shows, I've only had to ask two riders to leave the ring for this reason. One was horrified by what he had done and apologized immediately. He said his temper had gotten the better of him. I accepted his apology but forbade him from any further showing that day.

The other rider was even more abusive toward her horse in the ring. She repeatedly whipped and spurred her horse while yanking on his mouth and drawing blood around the bit. When I asked her to leave the ring, she started yelling at me, which effectively stopped the class. I requested a second time that she leave the ring and again she refused. At that point I called the manager to deal with the situation.

The manager had no more luck than I did getting her to leave the ring. If a person on a horse does not want to leave a ring, there's not much you can do to force him or her to leave. The manager and I conferred and decided to try a different maneuver: We told the other competitors in the ring that we couldn't finish the class until this rider left the ring. There is nothing like twenty people on horseback giving you dirty looks to get you in motion. The rider finally left the ring quietly and the class continued.

Most people do not intend to be unreasonable, but their emotions take over. You need to realize this problem and not feed into the situation and make it worse. Try to look at every issue from the viewpoint of the other person, which will help you explain things calmly and clearly. Your whole mission in dealing with disappointed riders is to be understanding and explain your position and decision in nonemotional terms. Most people are not looking for an argument; nor are they trying to display poor sportsmanship. Rather, they are honestly confused about why they received a lower ribbon than what they felt they deserved, or received none at all.

Some shows will ask permission to post your judge's cards so that competitors can look at them and see what they did wrong. Some judges allow their cards to be displayed, while others do not. I do not like my cards to be posted. I'm quite happy to explain one-on-one with a rider (with the steward present, of course) why he or she pinned a particular way.

Clix Photography

Last impressions count! This young rider has her lower leg forward during the final lineup, which is not a great last impression to leave with a judge.

I like to be able to explain my card one-on-one, because my symbols look like Swahili to most people. I've had nothing but trouble when I've allowed my cards to be posted. My handwriting is atrocious and some of my symbols are unusual, so it's hard for people to understand my thoughts. This in turn leads to many more people having questions than if the cards hadn't been posted. Even when I post my list of symbols and deductions, people still have a problem understanding my writing.

Many other judges, however, have no problems posting their cards. If you're comfortable posting your results, go for it. The competitors definitely like it when the cards are posted.

REPORTING PROBLEMS

Sometimes, no matter how hard you try, you cannot resolve a difficult situation. If this happens, you have several choices.

At a recognized show, ask to speak to the steward alone. Explain the issues and problems from your viewpoint. Ask for assistance in defusing the situation, and then both you and the steward can approach the person with the problem together. Most of the time, speaking quietly with the steward and the person who brought up the issue will resolve differences.

If the steward is unable to help you because of the irrationality of the competitor, trainer, or parent, the situation may have to be decided by the national organization that sanctions the show. At this point the steward will usually write up a report or the person doing the complaining will file a protest with the steward that will be sent to the organization. I've been very lucky in that I've never (knock wood) had an issue that couldn't be resolved on the show grounds. However, I know a few judges who have not been as lucky.

If a competitor, trainer, or parent is determined to take his or her opinion, however misguided, all the way to the organization headquarters, there is not much you can do about it. To prepare for the eventual hearing, take notes about the situation. Also, suggest the organization interview other competitors or trainers who witnessed the incident and/or disagreement.

Sometimes the judge must be the one to report a problem to the organization. If you have a situation in which your eyesight or parentage is being called into question and the steward cannot extract an apology from the perpetrator, you must be prepared to report the person and the situation. This can be done at the show by officially reporting the incident to the steward—who by this time is all too aware of the problem—and having the steward write it up and submit the report to the organization.

At an unrecognized show, the manager may be able to talk through the issue with the parties involved. Since there is usually less pressure at an unrecognized show than at a recognized show, the manager is usually successful in resolving conflict.

FINDING A REPLACEMENT JUDGE

No matter how much you think it might never happen to you, there will come a day when you will have to cancel your appearance at a show. It may be due to health reasons or a family emergency, but whatever the cause, you must give the show as much notice as possible.

If you are able to give the show several weeks' or months' notice, management should be able to find a replacement judge without too much trouble. Should you have to cancel the day before or the morning of the competition, you owe it to the show manager to help find another judge.

Recently I was scheduled to judge a schooling show on an early-spring Sunday morning. I woke up at three o'clock in the morning with the flu, complete with a sore throat and fever and chills. The show was going to start at nine o'clock, but I knew there was no way I would make it through a day of judging. At five-thirty I got on the phone to the show manager to explain how sick I was, and then proceeded to call every judge I knew within a hundred miles to see if someone could substitute for me.

Eventually a suitable substitute was found and the show went on. I was lucky in this case because a licensed official wasn't required at this schooling show, and a local unlicensed judge agreed to officiate. If it had been a recognized show, I would have had to find a licensed official to take over my duties.

WHAT HAPPENS WHEN A SHOW IS CANCELED?

Sometimes a show will have to cancel competition due to unforeseen circumstances, such as a problem with the location or a death in the family. For a judge, this is not a problem when it happens more than thirty days prior to the event; you can often book another show for that day.

I do have a problem, however, when the day before a show the manager feels that the event is not receiving enough entries to make a profit, so he or she cancels the competition. In this circumstance you are well within reason to request a cancellation fee of at least half your standard fee.

Sometimes, a show that is in progress must cancel due to such weather concerns as thunder and lightning. If the show has lasted less than half a day, I will reduce my fee in consideration of the circumstances.

Going on the Road

IF YOU'RE GOING TO JUDGE, you're going to have to travel. Traveling from show to show can be a wonderful experience, but you must be prepared to deal with the rigors of life on the road.

If you work at a large show that hosts more than one judge, you will probably find yourself staying at the same hotel as the other officials. You can then carpool to the show and have meals together. On the negative side, if you're tired of your coworkers at the end of a long day, you have nowhere to hide. I've never had this become a problem: When I'm tired and need my rest, I just excuse myself and go to my room.

Journeying to a different region of the country to judge is a great experience because you'll see new riders and horses and in a different atmosphere. It is also interesting to see how riders and horses vary from region to region. In one area of the country, for instance, riders might tend to ride with their stirrups too long or their lower legs too far forward compared to where you're from. Riding trends seem to become entrenched in one region because of the training available in that area. And although the riders may be different, your judging should remain consistent.

TIPS FOR TRAVELING

Traveling can be nerve-racking due to late flights, rental cars that break down, and noisy hotels. The key to staying sane is being organized ahead of time and being flexible when the time comes.

When you are contacted by a show that will require you to stay overnight, be very clear with the show about your needs. Many shows want to save money by having judges room together. If I don't know someone, however, I am not comfortable rooming with her no matter how nice she may seem. Also, I can no longer room with a smoker no matter how much I may like the person.

On the flip side, when I'm judging a multiday show, I go to bed disgustingly early every night, no later than 9 P.M. Therefore, rooming with someone who is a night owl is unfair to both of us. I'm happy to room with another judge if I've already made her acquaintance and I know we will be compatible in the same room for any length of time. And you never know when you may literally be stuck in a hotel. The great spring blizzard of 1993 canceled a horse show already in progress in Connecticut, causing judge Rita Timpanaro to spend a couple of extra days in a hotel room in the middle of nowhere. I was also at this show, and Rita and I spent a lot of quality time together. I managed to leave the day before Rita, but she had to soldier on alone until she could drive home.

In that regard, always plan for the worst. Bring extra clothes, a good book, your computer, and any medical prescriptions you may need. Your whole mission when traveling should be to keep things as simple as possible, but to be prepared for anything.

If you must fly in to a show, leave enough time on both ends of the trip so that you are not rushing to arrive at or leave the show. I've known several officials who booked flights home on a Sunday at 6 P.M. after a full day of judging. Unless a show is located at the airport, however, you cannot be assured that you will catch your flight. Even if the show ends at 4:30 P.M. and the airport is an hour away under ideal circumstances, there is no way you can catch that flight, especially now with more stringent airport security checks.

Unless you positively must be back at work at your regular job on Monday morning, plan to spend Sunday night at the show's location. It is unfair to the horse show and the competitors for you to rush on Sunday just because you need to catch a flight.

Some managers will want you to rent a car, while others will arrange for you to be picked up and delivered back to the airport. Whatever is decided, just be sure to confirm the plan at least three days before the show. If, at that point, plans have changed, you still have enough time to make alternative arrangements, such as renting a car. Be sure to save your rental receipts so the show can reimburse you.

Many friends refer to me as the Road Warrior because I would rather drive than fly to a show. Somehow, driving my own car when I'm in a strange town helps keep me centered and sane. It also allows me to take my clothes, computer, rule books, and, if the show doesn't object, my dog, Cookie.

Meals on the road can be a challenge, especially if you don't know the area. If you are on a restricted diet, such as vegetarian or kosher, make sure to do your research before you arrive, and let the show management know. Most managers are happy to provide you with suitable food on the show grounds, but you're on your own when you eat out at night. If the show does not provide meals but rather gives you a daily stipend for food, ask the local staff or other show officials for restaurant recommendations.

The Internet is a great assistance when I travel to a new area. You can look up ahead of time which services are available at your hotel, find local restaurants, locate the nearest medical clinic and other pertinent information. If there is incomplete information on the Internet, call your hotel and ask to speak to the concierge if the hotel employs one. Should you be staying at a small motel, check with the front desk staff for local amenities.

WHAT TO CHARGE FOR YOUR SERVICES AND TRAVELING

Only one person can decide what your time is worth as a judge, and that is you. Some people charge only a minimal amount to judge or just want their expenses covered because they either don't need the income or they just plain love to judge. Others, however, don't have that luxury.

Your licenses and qualifications as a judge have a great bearing on what you can charge, as does the region of the country you live in. USAE Registered judges can charge more for their services than Recorded judges, and Recorded judges can usually charge more than a

A ROUGH GUIDE TO FEES

The following fees should be used only as a general guide when thinking about what your rates should be to judge. As mentioned earlier, you need to take into consideration your qualifications, the location of the show, and the type of judging you will be doing. For instance, many shows pay a trail judge less money because the trail judge usually has a shorter day than other officials.

The fees suggested will vary and do not include expenses such as mileage and food. Prices quoted are per day, and may vary with a show that runs for multiple days.

4-H shows	$150–300, depending on the size of the show and what is charged for entry fees
Schooling and open shows	$150–400
Intercollegiate shows	$250–400
Recognized shows	$250–600

judge with no license. There are some shows, however, that pay each judge the same amount no matter what his or her qualifications are. Still, at the majority of shows each judge is paid according to licenses and qualifications.

An area of the country that is dense in judges, such as Western judges in Texas or Hunter/Jumper judges in the Northeast, will have more competition for jobs. Hence, the amount you can charge may be set by the market rather than by your pocketbook. Prices vary from region to region—and it all depends on the pool of talent in your area.

Some shows will pay a per diem for food, while others reimburse for the actual cost of meals. As far as mileage goes, I've been paid a low of ten cents a mile, and a high of thirty-four cents a mile. I think fair is somewhere around thirty cents a mile. (The current IRS rate is 34½ cents.) Tolls are additional and not included in the mileage fee.

If you must travel a day to the show and another day to get back home, don't expect to be paid for your travel days. I have yet to find a show that pays for them. Is this fair? Perhaps not, but that's the way it is.

To be honest, I charge different rates for various horse shows. If I'm invited to judge a local 4-H show, my fee is going to be different from when I'm asked to judge a large recognized show. My rate is also going to be different for a show that has steadily employed me and supported me for years, as opposed to a show where I have never worked before. And my rate is certainly different for a show that I know is a pain in the butt to judge (the hassle factor), rather than a show that is fun to go to.

When deciding on your rates, take everything into account—your experience, qualifications, licenses, and the hassle factor—to come to a fair decision. And never be afraid to be flexible. Sometimes shows truly can't afford to pay you more than they are offering. It is then up to you to decide if it is worth your time to judge the show.

Keeping Your License Current and Moving Up

WITH A LITTLE BIT OF LUCK and a tremendous amount of hard work, you've hopefully had the opportunity to judge many different types of horse shows over a three- to five-year span. After such experience will come the time to think about whether or not you want to maintain your license and maybe even apply for a promotion.

REQUIREMENTS TO KEEP YOUR LICENSE

Your work is not over after you have obtained your license. You must then fulfill certain requirements to keep it. Depending on the organization, you must judge a specified number of recognized shows within a certain time frame and attend licensed judges' clinics every two to five years. Additionally, some breeds and disciplines require a passing mark on a written test every few years. Failure to fulfill these requirements will result in losing your license.

The suggestions listed earlier in this book should result in at least one officiating opportunity within the time frame. However, if you are not willing to sacrifice, work hard, or compromise your standards to get a job, you will have a tough time. A judge's license is a privilege, not a right. You need to work to get it, and you need to work to keep it.

Many people do the minimum amount of work just to stay licensed, because they feel having a judge's card adds to their careers as trainers, instructors, or riders. Others like to keep their card because they feel they get more jobs at schooling shows because of it. Either way, your license is a valuable commodity and should not be given up lightly. If you do give up your license and later decide to get it again, you will have to repeat all the steps and work that went into obtaining it the first time.

Moral: Unless you are firm in your belief that you are giving up judging for good, maintain the requirements and keep your license current.

ARE YOU READY FOR PROMOTION?

After officiating as an entry-level judge for several years, you may decide to try for a promotion. This decision is not to be made lightly. For instance, many USAE Recorded judges stay busy and productive judging numerous shows, and they never feel the urge to upgrade to Registered status. Why? Because sometimes Recorded judges who are promoted to Registered status will actually get fewer shows to judge, similar to when they first got their Recorded status and had to struggle to find jobs. Once you have jumped up a level, you need to prove yourself all over again.

To apply for your promotion means you need to follow the specific requirements of your chosen organization. Each organization lists the number of recognized competitions to be judged within a specified number of years before you can apply for your promotion. You must also attend judges' clinics as specified, and you may need a passing score on an examination.

As when you initially applied to become a judge, type your application so it presents a professional appearance and enclose a check for the required fee. As with other important documents, it is a good idea to send it certified mail, return receipt requested.

Judge Timothy Cleary marks his card with results during the final lineup.

Simply fulfilling the organization's requirements is not enough to earn a promotion. It is always better to go beyond the minimum requirements. Gain as much experience as possible, and continue to make connections within the show world. The better known and respected you are, the better your chances of promotion. Once again, volunteer your time at shows, help with Pony Club and 4-H events, and find other ways to let people become familiar with your name and abilities.

That's because your background and judging experience must demonstrate to the Licensed Officials Committee that you are prepared to handle the added responsibility of becoming a higher-rated judge. As when you first applied for your license, the Licensed Officials Committee will send out questionnaires and invite comment on your qualifications. Your chances of getting a promotion are slim if your name is not familiar to anyone on the Licensed Officials Committee and you have not put enough energy into advancing yourself as a judge and horseman.

Getting a promotion is very difficult and may take many years, because standards are kept very high to maintain judging quality and consistency. If you are rejected on your first application, go out and obtain more experience, and then apply again after a few years. There is no specified waiting time before reapplying, but it behooves you to judge many additional shows and gain more experience prior to trying again.

Personally, I've never felt the desire to apply for a promotion. I receive many calls to judge all types of horse shows without having a USAE Registered judge's card (I hold a Recorded judge's status). I'm honored to judge a variety of horse shows with the licenses I hold, and I feel no need at this point in my life to go further. A few years down the road, however, I may feel differently.

JUDGING LARGER HORSE SHOWS

If you've applied for and received a promotion in your chosen breed or discipline, congratulations! For some people, a promotion is the ticket to judging the big-time shows.

Although the larger USAE shows usually only want to hire someone with an "R" card, sometimes they can hire a judge who only has an "r" for certain rings and duties. This has been the case for me. In the past few years, I've been privileged to judge at the Sugarbush Horse Show, the Valley Classic, and the Gold Coast Classic, all USAE A-rated Hunter/Jumper shows. Although I haven't judged the Regular Working Hunters or the "big" equitation classes like the USAE Medal or the ASPCA Maclay, I have been able to judge many interesting classes with phenomenal horses and riders, and I've enjoyed the opportunity to work with some wonderful judges. This sort of experience helps you grow as an official and as a horseman.

Generally, being asked to judge at a larger horse show means a greater commitment on your part. The larger and more prestigious a horse show is, the longer it lasts. With many of these shows, you will end up being away from home for a week or more at a time.

If you accept a judging assignment at a large, multiday show, be prepared to work much harder than at a small show. Classes at the big shows will often have more than thirty horses each. I've judged Pre-Green Hunters at some of these shows that had more than seventy entries! When you are faced with judging a class this large, you've got to be prepared in several different ways.

First, get enough rest each night. This may seem like a no-brainer, but often judges end up going out to eat with one another and find themselves staying up late talking. If you are going out to eat, ensure that you have your own means of transportation so that you can leave if it starts to get late. There is nothing worse than being trapped at a restaurant because you didn't drive your own vehicle. Getting enough rest is especially important when you find yourself still judging at seven in the evening because the show management added some classes in your ring. You need to be sharp to judge, and getting enough rest helps you stay that way.

Stay focused and stay organized. When you are judging large numbers of horses, it is easy to allow some things to escape your notice if you are not careful. This is the time to make sure that your bookkeeping system can keep track of both the best and the worst of what you see.

Whether you are judging seventy horses over fences or seventy reining horses in a row, you must be ready for them to come at you quickly, one after another. Often, when I'm judging horses or riders over fences, the one in the ring will be finishing over his final fence while the next entry is already trotting into the ring. You've got to assign scores quickly in such instances or you have no hope of keeping track of what is going on. In addition, you must keep a current list of your top placings at any given time in case your announcer is looking to broadcast a standby list of the top entries.

If you're judging an A horse show, the competitors have paid a lot of money and invested a lot of time to be there. Not only do you need to act like a professional, you need to look the part, too. Although you should have a suitable judge's wardrobe by the time you're asked to officiate at an A show, this is definitely the time to upgrade your look if you have any doubts. As at smaller shows, men should wear a suit and tie. For women, classic and simple dress suits or pantsuits are the way to go. The outfit doesn't have to be made by Prada, but you should look your best and ensure that your

Judges dressed appropriately for judging a prestigious national show. Anne Lawter, Lisa Cunningham Waller, and Richard M. Sereni at the 2001 Morgan Grand National.

outfit is pressed and creased (the only time I iron anymore is when I'm judging the next day).

Very few judges actually get the opportunity to judge at the best shows in their chosen discipline. Be prepared to work hard, but also remember the reasons you began judging in the first place—your love of horses and the sport.

A Final Word

I HAD VISIONS OF GLAMOUR AND GLORY when I decided to become a judge. Since then, I have found that a judge's life more often resembles an equine cartoon strip. Unusual competitors, biting ponies, rickety viewing stands, and backwoods bathrooms are all a part of my world.

But between the long hours, hot dusty rings, and sometimes unusual competitors, there is no better way to spend a day than as a horse show judge. It doesn't matter what type of show I'm judging; I always learn something new and take away a feeling of satisfaction.

I hope that after reading this book you'll want to start judging yourself. And if you decide judging isn't for you, I hope that you've at least learned a bit about judging that will help you in your show career. Remember, a judge sees every trick in the book, so to speak, and knowing this can improve your showing skills.

My judging occurs mostly at smaller USAE and schooling shows. This is truly work in the trenches, not at glamorous shows. But I would not trade the friendships, good times, and learning experiences of these shows for anything. After all these years, I still get excited when I go to judge a horse show.

In the meantime, help feed and spay or neuter the barn cats, ride well, play fair, and have fun!

Glossary of Common Judging and Show Terms

Big "R" A USAE Registered judge.

Breeches (pronounced *britches*) Riding pants for Hunter Seat riders that are designed to be worn with high boots.

Canter or Lope A three-beat gait. The canter has either a left or right lead. The order of leg movement for a right lead is off-side rear, then the diagonal pair of off-side foreleg with near-side rear, and finally the near-side foreleg. For the left lead, the order is near-side rear, then the diagonal near-side foreleg with off-side rear leg, and finally the off-side foreleg.

Card The term *card* has two meanings. First, the word is used to refer to the licenses a judge holds ("he is carded in Stock Seat Equitation"). It can also refer to the piece of paper that the judge marks with results during a class.

Chaps Leather leggings for Stock Seat riders that cover and protect the legs. Chaps fasten around the waist, and then cover the legs from hips to ankles.

Class List The list of classes in a show.

Coach A person who instructs riders in the art of showing, at shows and at home. Also called a trainer.

Conformation The horse's physical characteristics compared to the breed's ideal.

Cross-Rails Small fences used in beginner classes over fences. Two rails are crossed to create a low X in the center of the jump, hence the name *cross-rails*.

Danish System A 4-H method of judging where riders are ranked by individual standards of performance rather than ranking them against other riders.

Diagonal   The post of the rider at the trot, depending on the direction of travel. When moving in a clockwise fashion, the rider posts in time with the outside (in this case left) shoulder and should be on the left diagonal. This means the rider should be in the "up" portion of the post when the outside shoulder is forward, and sitting down when the outside shoulder swings back.

Division   A collection of related classes at a show together make up a division.

Equitation Class   A class in which the rider is judged on horsemanship, position, and control of the horse.

Faults   A fault is a penalty during the performance of a horse. In Jumper classes common faults include refusals, knockdowns, and exceeding the time allowed. In Hunter classes faults can include poor movement and jumping form. In Western Pleasure classes faults include holding the head too high or pinning the ears.

Frame   The posture in which a horse holds himself while demonstrating his gaits.

Gaits   The different movements and ways of moving forward of the horse on the flat. These include the walk, trot/jog, canter/lope, and hand gallop.

Good Mover   A horse that covers the ground in a way pleasing to the judge's eye.

Hand   The unit of equine measurement equal to four inches.

Hand Gallop   The three-beat gait that is faster than a canter/lope and slower than a gallop.

Hunter Classes   A class in which the horse is judged on his jumping form, ability, overall appearance, manners, and movement under saddle ("way of going").

In-Hand Classes   Classes in which the handler is unmounted and shows the horse in a halter or bridle.

Jodhpurs   Ankle-length pants for riding, generally worn with paddock or jodhpur boots.

Jog or Trot   A two-beat gait in which the horse's legs work in diagonal pairs, left front with right rear and right front with left rear. Hunter Seat riders generally post to the trot, while Stock Seat riders usually sit the jog.

Jump Courses   A group of fences that is jumped in a specific order, a "course" of fences.

Jumpers   A division in which the horse is judged on time and jumping faults only.

Leads   See *Canter*.

Lineup   The entries' standing in a row at the end of the class for the final inspection by the judge.

Little "r"   A USAE Recorded judge.

Lope   See *Canter*.

Movement   The manner in which the horse moves under saddle at the walk, trot, and canter is referred to as movement.

Near Side   The left side of the horse.

Off Side   The right side of the horse.

On Deck   The next rider waiting to go in the ring is on deck.

On the Flat   When Hunter Seat Equitation riders are judged at the walk, trot, and canter.

Over Fences   Any Equitation or Hunter class in which a course of fences is jumped.

Pinning   The act of the judge placing the class in the order in which ribbons will be awarded.

Pleasure Class   A class in which the horse is judged on his ability to give a good pleasure ride. The horse must move evenly, be mannerly, and act sensibly. Further requirements vary from discipline to discipline and breed to breed.

Ponies   Certain breeds of small equines. Ponies are separated into three different sizes for most horse show purposes: small (under 12.2 hands), medium (over 12.2 up to 13.2 hands), and large (over 13.2 up to 14.2 hands).

Posting   The act of rising and sitting in rhythm with the horse's trot for Hunter Seat riders (see *Diagonal*).

Prize List   See *Class List*.

Ratcatcher   A riding shirt with a high collar and choker.

Rating   Shows are separated by size and prize money offered, and are "rated" in this manner.

Refusals   A horse stopping or running out instead of jumping a designated fence or obstacle on a course.

Schooling Show   A show that is not rated by any organization, held to give people experience in showing.

Seat   The manner in which a rider sits on the horse.

Short-Stirrup Division   A group of classes for young riders, usually under the age of thirteen.

Spotting   A competitor's making eye contact with a judge in Showmanship or Fitting and Showing classes.

Striding   The distance between fences on a course, measured in a horse's strides.

Tack   The equipment used on the horse to ride and control it, such as saddles, bridles, and halters.

Trail Course   A group of related obstacles that are ridden in a certain order.

Trainer   See *Coach*.

Trot   See *Jog*.

Turnout   The appearance and finish of a horse and rider.

Under Saddle   A non-jumping class in a Hunter Division in which a hunter performs at the walk, trot, and canter, and is judged on his movement and manners.

Walk   The slowest of the gaits; it is a four-beat gait. The legs work in the order of near-side rear, near-side foreleg, off-side rear, then off-side foreleg.

International, National, and Regional Show Organizations That License or Approve Judges

American Buckskin Registry
    Association (ABRA)
P.O. Box 3850
Redding, CA 96049
(530) 223-1420
www.americanbuckskin.org

American Donkey & Mule Society
    (ADMS)
P.O. Box 1210
Lewisville, TX 75067
(972) 219-0781 phone
(972) 420-9980 fax
adms@juno.com
www.geocities.com/lovelongears/

The American Driving Society (ADS)
Box 160
Metamora, MI 48455
(810) 664-8666 phone
(810) 664-2405 fax
info@americandrivingsociety.org
www.americandrivingsociety.org

American Horse Shows Association –
    see USA Equestrian

American Miniature Horse Association
    (AMHA)
5601 South Interstate 35W
Alvarado, TX 76009
(817) 783-5600
information@amha.org
www.amha.com
www.minihorses.com

American Morgan Horse Association
   (AMHA)
P.O. Box 960
Shelburne, VT 05482
(802) 985-4944 phone
(802) 985-8897 fax
www.morganhorse.com

American Paint Horse Association
   (APHA)
P.O. Box 961023
Fort Worth, TX 76161-0023
(817) 834-APHA phone
(817) 834-3152 fax
www.apha.com

American Quarter Horse Association
   (AQHA)
P.O. Box 200
Amarillo, TX 79168
(806) 376-4811
www.aqha.org

The American Shetland Pony
   Club/TheAmerican Miniature
   Horse Registry
81 B Queenwood Road
Morton, IL 61550
(309) 263-4044 phone
(309) 263-5113 fax
info@shetlandminiature.com
www.shetlandminiature.com

Appaloosa Horse Club (ApHC)
2720 West Pullman Road
Moscow, ID 83843
(208) 882-5578 phone
(208) 882-8150 fax
aphc@appaloosa.com
www.appaloosa.com

Canadian Equestrian Federation (CEF)
2460 Lancaster Road
Ottawa, Ontario K1B 4S5
(613) 248-3433 phone
(613) 248-3484 fax
www.equinecanada.com

Color Breed Council (CBC)
P.O. Box 161995
Fort Worth, TX 76161
(817) 335-6632 phone
(817) 336-7416 fax
www.colorbreedcouncil.com

Fédération Equestre Internationale
   (FEI)
Avenue Mon Repos 24
P.O. Box 157
1000 Lausanne 5, Switzerland
41 21 310 47 47 phone
41 21 310 47 60 fax
info@horsesport.org
www.horsesport.org

Intercollegiate Horse Shows
   Association (IHSA)
P.O. Box 108
Fairfield, CT 06430
(203) 259-5100 phone
(203) 256-9377 fax
www.ihsa.com

International Andalusian and Lusitano
   Horse Association (IALHA)
101 Carnoustie North, Suite 200
Birmingham, AL 35242
(205) 995-8900 phone
(205) 995-8966 fax
office@ialha.com
www.ialha.org

International Arabian Horse
   Association (IAHA)
10805 East Bethany Drive
Aurora, CO 80014
(303) 696-4500
www.iaha.com

International Buckskin Horse
  Association (IBHA)
P.O. Box 268
Shelby, IN 46377
(219) 552-1013
IBHA@netnitco.net
www.ibha.net

National Cutting Horse Association
  (NCHA)
4704 Highway 377 South
Fort Worth, TX 76116-8805
(817) 244-6188
www.nchacutting.com

National Disability Sports Alliance
  (NDSA)
25 West Independence Way
Kingston, RI 02881
(401) 792-7130 phone
(401) 792-7132 fax
info@ndsaonline.org or
  equestrian@ndsaonline.org
www.ndsaonline.org

National Miniature Donkey
  Association (NMDA)
3535 Nicolaus Road
Lincoln, CA 95648
(916) 645-9606

National Reined Cowhorse
  Association (NRCHA)
4500 South Laspina Street, Suite 224
Tulare, CA 93274
(559) 687-3222 phone
(559) 687-3223 fax
www.nrcha.com

National Reining Horse Association
  (NRHA)
3000 Northwest 10th Street
Oklahoma City, OK 73107-5302
(405) 946-7400
www.nrha.com

National Show Horse Registry
10368 Bluegrass Parkway
Louisville, KY 40299
(502) 266-5100 phone
(502) 266-5806 fax
nshowhorse@aol.com
www.nshregistry.org

National Snaffle Bit Association
  (NSBA)
4815 South Sheridan, Suite 109
Tulsa, OK 74145
(918) 270-1469 phone
(918) 270-1471 fax
www.nsba.com

New England Horsemen's Council
  (NEHC)
P.O. Box 70
Sandown, NH 03873
(603) 887-NEHC phone
(603) 887-5252 fax
nehc28@hotmail.com
www.nehc.info

North American Riding for the
  Handicapped
P.O. Box 33150
Denver, CO 80233
(800) 369-RIDE phone
(303) 252-4610 fax
narha@narha.org
www.narha.org

Palomino Horse Breeders Association
  (PHBA)
15253 East Skelly Drive
Tulsa, OK 74116-2637
(918) 438-1234 phone
(918) 438-1232 fax
yellahrses@aol.com
www.palominohba.com

Pinto Horse Association of America, Inc.
1900 Samuels Avenue
Fort Worth, TX 76102-1141
(817) 336-7842 phone
(817) 336-7416 fax
www.pinto.org

Pony of the Americas Club, Inc. (POAC)
5240 Elmwood Avenue
Indianapolis, IN 46203
(317) 788-0107 phone
(317) 788-8974 fax
poac@poac.org
www.poac.org

USA Equestrian (USAE) (formerly AHSA)
4047 Iron Works Parkway
Lexington, KY 40511
(859) 258-2472 phone
(859) 231-6662 fax
www.equestrian.org

United States Dressage Federation (USDF)
220 Lexington Green Circle, Suite 500
Lexington, KY 40503
(859) 971-2277 phone
(859) 971-7722 fax
usdressage@usdf.org
www.usdf.org

Index